Nicholas II

*A Captivating Guide to the Last Emperor of
Russia and How the Romanov Dynasty
Collapsed as a Result of the Russian
Revolution*

Free Bonus from Captivating History
(Available for a Limited time)

Hi History Lovers!

Now you have a chance to join our exclusive history list so you can get your first history ebook for free as well as discounts and a potential to get more history books for free! Simply visit the link below to join.

Captivatinghistory.com/ebook

Also, make sure to follow us on Facebook, Twitter and Youtube by searching for Captivating History.

Contents

FREE BONUS FROM CAPTIVATING HISTORY (AVAILABLE FOR A LIMITED TIME) 1

INTRODUCTION 3

CHAPTER 1 – THE EARLY LIFE OF THE TSAR 5

CHAPTER 2 – THE LAST TSAR'S RISE TO POWER 15

CHAPTER 3 – THE RUSSO-JAPANESE WAR AND THE MASSACRE OF BLOODY SUNDAY 24

CHAPTER 4 – NICHOLAS'S REFORMS AND THE INTRODUCTION OF RASPUTIN 33

CHAPTER 5 – NICHOLAS II AND THE ONSET OF THE GREAT WAR...42

CHAPTER 6 – THE FALL OF GRIGORI RASPUTIN: RUSSIA'S SCAPEGOAT AND THE ROMANOVS' TRUSTED ADVISOR.....................51

CHAPTER 7 – THE FINAL YEARS FOR NICHOLAS II AS TSAR OF RUSSIA 59

CHAPTER 8 – FROM TSAR TO CITIZEN: THE ABDICATION OF NICHOLAS II...67

CHAPTER 9 – A COUNTRY IN TRANSITION AND THE ROMANOVS' ARREST 73

CHAPTER 10 – THE EXECUTION OF NICHOLAS II AND THE ROMANOV FAMILY 81

CONCLUSION: THE LEGACY OF NICHOLAS II 91

BIBLIOGRAPHY 96

Introduction

"I have a firm, an absolute conviction that the fate of Russia—that my own fate and that of my family—is in the hands of God who has placed me where I am. Whatever may happen to me, I shall bow to His will with the consciousness of never having had any thought other than that of serving the country which He has entrusted to me."

-Tsar Nicholas II

Tsar Nicholas II is a complicated and controversial figure in Russian history. His rule came on the heels of his autocratic father's death, and his succession to the throne led to a revolving door of conflicts, from a brutal and bloody coronation to the eventual collapse of the Romanov family as a whole through the efforts of the Russian Revolution. As Nicholas II was such a crucial figure in shaping Russia, he deserves further inspection into his story of what guided him, what hindered him, and what led him to serve as the face of the total collapse of the over 300-year-old imperial dynasty.

In fact, Tsar Nicholas II's life ended in such an abrupt and violent manner that historians would wonder about the details for years after the event. Not only did the tale of Nicholas II lead to an enigmatic assassination of an entire family, but it also marked a distinct turning point for the history of Russia that affected the rest of the world. To understand the catalysts leading up to the final execution of an entire royal family, though, it's important to step back and observe how Nicholas went from a cherished heir to the Russian throne to the last tsar that Russia would ever know.

Chapter 1 – The Early Life of the Tsar

When Nikolai Alexandrovich Romanov was born on May 6th, 1868, he seemed to have the whole world laid out before him. His father, Alexander Alexandrovich, better known as Alexander III, and his mother, Danish Princess Maria Feodorovna, celebrated his birth both with the excitement of new parents and as rulers who would need an heir to the Russian throne.

The reign of Nicholas, unbeknownst to Russia at the time, would mark the end of a political era and serve as the final chapter of a revolution. However, as the fall of the Romanovs was a far-off concept at the time of his birth, Nicholas was celebrated, just as any new heir to the throne would be. He quickly became the favorite grandchild of the current tsar, Alexander II, and was considered an asset to the royal family.

In his early life, due to the efforts of his mother and the luxuries that a royal life offered, Nicholas lived comfortably. Generally, the young royal wanted for nothing and received the best that Russia had to offer in the form of private tutors.

The young royal Nicholas showed proficiency in foreign languages and history but reportedly struggled with other subjects, such as economics and politics. This discrepancy in his education would come back to haunt him later once he took on the mantle of tsar and assumed responsibility for Russia. Although Nicholas would later show that foreign affairs were his strength as a leader, his struggle to grasp the internal political climate of Russia would lead him to make grave mistakes he would never recover from.

One tutor the tsarevich had was a man named Konstantin Petrovich Pobedonostsev, who had also taught Nicholas's father. He influenced both of their philosophies with his teachings and would lead them to ideas that negatively affected their relationship with the Russian people and eventually lead to general social discontent. He is widely considered to be one of the most influential members of the tsar's court during the reigns of both Alexander III and Nicholas II.

Pobedonostsev claimed to believe in two things above all else: the Russian Orthodox Church and autocracy. This was based on a harsh lesson he passed down to both Alexander III and Nicholas II. He told both men that God gave the tsar his power and position. As such, if someone denied God, they denied the tsar, and if someone doubted the tsar, they denied God. Pobedonostsev's beliefs would even earn him the nickname "The High Priest of Social Stagnation."

The tutor would pass down lessons to his pupils that were steeped in his belief in autocracy. His bigotry often shown in these teachings as well. He would frequently refer to other races as lazy and sluggish in lengthy tirades. Pobedonostsev was also the effective minister of religion, which gave him the power to wield his religious bigotry harshly through the advisement of policies, such as a set of temporary laws enacted by Alexander III, known as the May Laws. These laws restricted Jewish people from settling in certain places, ranging from rural areas to the whole of the Pale of Settlement, the western region of the Russian Empire. The philosopher looked down harshly on anyone who stood against or wouldn't convert to Russian Orthodoxy. And the more strongly they resisted conversion to the Russian Orthodox Church, the more harshly Pobedonostsev looked down upon them. This led to a view rife with anti-Semitism and bigotry against Polish Catholics and Muslim individuals. This was particularly harmful in such a large country, as Russia was, of course, no stranger to a diverse demographic of citizens.

When it came to reformation, Pobedonostsev held no desire for the liberal approaches that catered to the preferences of the lower class, something that was no doubt linked to his high regard for autocracy. He once referred to the entire practice of social reform as, "This whole bazaar of projects...this noise of cheap and shallow ecstasies."

In more specific settings, his rhetoric only became harsher. When he was asked about the free press, he called it an "instrument of mass corruption." On the topic of universal suffrage, he said it was "a fatal error." Even on the topic of a constitution, like the one France had, he referred to them as a "fundamental evil."

In one of his longer tirades, Pobedonostsev would go on to attack the idea of parliaments, which was something some of the Russian people wanted so they could have more representation in their government. He stated:

> Among the falsest of political principles is the principle of the sovereignty of the people...which has unhappily infatuated certain foolish Russians...Parliament is an institution serving for the satisfaction of the personal ambition, vanity, a self-interest of its members. The institution of Parliament is indeed one of the greatest illustrations of human delusion...Providence has preserved our Russia, with its heterogeneous racial composition, from like misfortunes. It is terrible to think of our condition if destiny had sent us the fatal gift—an all-Russian Parliament. But that will never be.

It's important to note that this is the environment in which Nicholas grew up. These are the ideas that were presented to him from a young age. Even his later distaste for his father's personality and methods wasn't enough to stop him from internalizing this rhetoric and adopting his own ideas and opinions steeped in bigotry. Thus, the aggressive level of nationalism, racism, and religious intolerance of the people around Nicholas would lead him to continue philosophies that the Romanovs had held for years, which would ultimately negatively affect the relationship he held with the people of Russia.

Of course, this isn't to say that all forms of prejudice evaporated with the Romanov line, but it does highlight that these were concepts that Nicholas was introduced to early in his life and would carry throughout his years, later affecting how he behaved as tsar.

In 1881, young Nicholas would experience a stark sign of political unrest in Russia that would strike his family specifically. Throughout his early childhood, Russia was under the rule of his grandfather, Tsar Alexander II. However, on the morning of March 13th, 1881, while Tsar Alexander II and his royal entourage were chauffeured through St. Petersburg, an organization known as Narodnaya Volya (translated into English as "People's Will") was responsible for throwing a bomb at the tsar's carriage.

This was one group that was determined to overthrow the autocracy of the Russian monarchy and wasn't hesitant to meet their goals through harsh means, such as the assassinations of high-ranking officials. They were specifically angry at some of the methods of governmental reform of Alexander II. While he is well known in history for reforms such as relieving the oppression of the serfs, he was still an autocrat. When a revolutionary cause that he didn't agree with cropped up, he would crush them with the strength of a man who was used to wielding absolute power. To revolutionaries, this still made him a symbol of governmental oppression. This group would later lead to the rise of the Russian Socialist Revolutionary Party in the early 20th century.

By a miraculous turn of events, the tsar was relatively unharmed by the first bomb and even left his carriage to check on the other members of his entourage. Yet, in a renewed effort, a second assailant threw another bomb toward the now-unprotected tsar. This time, the bomb landed directly at the feet of Alexander II and ended in fatal injuries. This included the almost total loss of the tsar's left leg, a grave injury to his abdomen, and the deliverance of an alarming amount of shrapnel to his face. The tsar, realizing the gravity of the situation, commanded his party to return him to the palace to allow him, by his own words, "to die there." He then fell unconscious and remained that way for the journey home.

Once he arrived at the palace, the Romanov family was thrown into a frenzy. His family went immediately to his side in the vain hopes of restoring him or, at the very least, say their goodbyes to the tsar before it was too late. As for little Nicholas, he followed his grandfather's trail of blood from the entry of the palace to the room where he lay dying. Upon his arrival, Alexander III grabbed his son and pulled him close to the dying patriarch in an attempt to rouse his father a final time, pleading to him and saying, "Papa, your ray of sunshine is here."

Sadly, even the sight of his beloved grandson wasn't enough. By some accounts, the tsar seemed to try and sit up, raised a hand toward his family, and then collapsed back onto his bed and died without sharing any departing words. Shortly after, his physician officially declared him dead.

This tragic event set the stage for the next tsar, Nicholas's father, Alexander III. It was under his rule that the future Tsar Nicholas would grow to be the leader he was until the fall of the Romanovs. A part of what led to the building unrest in Russia, which would eventually lead to the total fall of the Romanov dynasty, was the strict and severe image that Alexander III would build. The death of Alexander II also triggered deep unrest in the country, as well as thrust Nicholas II onto a throne that he wasn't adequately prepared to hold.

Despite the shortcomings that made the Russians tire of Tsar Alexander II's rule, he was, generally speaking, the last reformer that the Russian Empire would see under the Romanovs. This is especially true in contrast to the actions of his son and grandson. For instance, it was Tsar Alexander II that would end serfdom in Russia, which had previously allowed the Russian upper class to use the lower class as forced labor.

Even on the day of his death, Tsar Alexander II was working on reform. Specifically, he was pushing for the creation of the Loris-Melikov's constitution. This brand-new constitution aimed to offer the lower class even more liberation from the heavy and oppressive hand of the upper class. Unfortunately, for the assassinating group, these reforms came too little too late. Instead of promoting the revolutionary change that they'd hoped for, the Romanovs simply continued the line of succession by appointing Alexander III.

For the lower class, these hopes were destroyed the minute Alexander III took power as the new tsar. Tsar Alexander III saw the unrest in Russia, and rather than seeing an uprising lower class who was dissatisfied with their subservience as the source of it, he blamed his father's liberal and "soft" approach as the cause. In turn, the new tsar set out to create a hard example and force Russia back into a state of peace. He was once quoted as saying that he was determined that the masses of Russia would "feel the whip" of his rule.

As tsar, Alexander III was also the antithesis of his father when it came to talking about reforms. Alexander II had been more prone to start a dialogue with his people and his advisors when it came to creating and implementing policies. For Alexander III, a dialogue could only start if it was led by him and if it was in line with his beliefs and dictations. Alexander III was quicker to follow his own opinion above anyone else's, and he even verbally or physically abused those around him. And he wasn't limited to talking down to just the lower class either. In one fairly infamous dispute, one of the tsar's advisors threatened to resign over his policies. Upon receiving the official's resignation, the tsar knocked the man down. When the official protested to the abusive treatment, the tsar bellowed at the injured man, "Shut up! When I choose to kick you out, you will hear of it in no uncertain terms!"

In his youth, Nicholas was actually the opposite of his father. While his father was determined to show brutal strength, Nicholas was still reeling from the loss of his beloved grandfather and was fairly horrified at the policies his father put in place to undo what Tsar Alexander II had done to liberate the lower class and inspire reform in the country. Alexander III's harsh and abusive behavior to the people around him was also a nightmarish image to the young heir to the throne.

In his studies and personality, Nicholas was much more restrained and sensitive than his father. The young royal preferred to spend his time reading poetry and dedicating time to the arts, as opposed to his father, who showed more interest in military tactics and bringing his authoritarianism to the masses. While his father implemented strict policies, Nicholas was more concerned about having piles of books on hand for candlelight reading and ensuring he saved enough time for afternoon walks.

Even in their physical appearance, the tsar and his son seemed to be opposites. While Alexander III was a beast of a man at an impressive height of 6'3", his son would only ever reach the height of 5'7". This was a contributing factor in the state of their relationship because, as many authoritarians thought throughout history, Alexander III considered brute force and personal physicality as a crucial part of his presence as a ruler. There are even stories of the tsar showing forces of strength at gatherings, such as demonstrating his ability to bend a fireplace poker with his bare hands.

Conversely, Nicholas wasn't a tower of physical prowess. He was even noted to shrink back at the sight of his father when he was in his presence. While this difference in physicality may not have meant much to another ruler, it was yet another sign to Alexander III that his son was weak, and to an authoritarian leader such as him, this affected both their personal relationship and how Alexander treated Nicholas as the next leader of Russia.

The most telling example that would affect Nicholas when he later took the throne was the step of Alexander III excluding him from political life. While Nicholas would write in his diary about attending meetings of the Russian Imperial Council, his father mostly failed to prepare him for life as the tsar. Unlike many of the heirs that came before him, Nicholas didn't spend excessive time with his father learning what went into ruling a country like Russia.

That being said, the two men weren't complete opposites. Many of the evidence-backed accusations that were labeled to the current tsar would apply to Nicholas as well. This included tendencies of anti-Semitism and racial tensions toward Germans, despite the fact that Nicholas would take a German princess as his bride later in life.

Despite the rivalry and contempt that Alexander III generally held for his son, Nicholas was still the rightful heir to the Russian throne. As such, in 1884, at sixteen years old, Nicholas participated in his coming of age ceremony. It was held at the Russian Winter Palace, which was the official residence of the monarchs from 1732 to 1917. In the ceremony, not only was Nicholas recognized for his age, but he also recited a pledge of loyalty to his father as the tsar and committed to an oath to take on the mantle of tsar himself one day.

1884 was an important year in Nicholas's life for more than just his coming of age ceremony, as this was also the year that he would meet German Princess Alexandra Feodorovna. In the future, she would serve both as the young monarch's bride and fulfill the role of the last empress of Russia.

The two met when Alexandra was attending her sister Elizabeth's marriage in Russia. Elizabeth was set to marry another member of the royal family, namely Nicholas's uncle. The two were also second cousins. At the time, this was fairly common, as royal families were often married to one another in the formation of alliances and through marriages of convenience rather than the romantic love behind many modern marriages. Despite this trend of marriages of convenience at the time, Nicholas and Alexandra showed a genuine fondness for each other almost from the moment they first met.

It was noted that during her time in Russia, Nicholas and Alexandra became nearly inseparable. With similar backgrounds and upbringings, the two bonded quickly and spent much of their days on walks together and generally enjoying one another's presence. However, after her sister's marriage, Alexandra had to return to her position in Germany, and the two wouldn't see each other again for another five years. Upon their parting, Nicholas gifted Alexandra a piece of expensive jewelry as a memento to remember him and their time together. When they met again, it seemed that the German princess hadn't forgotten her fast friend from years before.

In 1889, the German princess returned to Russia to stay, once again, with her sister Elizabeth in St. Petersburg. Despite the long absence from one another, Nicholas and Alexandra quickly fell back into their routine together and became seemingly inseparable. Now that Nicholas was twenty-one, it didn't take long for him to woo the princess, but they wouldn't wed quite yet.

During this time, and through much of monarchical history, religion played a large role in the marriages of royal family members. Before their marriage, Alexandra was a Lutheran Protestant by faith, which clashed with the Russian Orthodox beliefs held by Nicholas and all of Russia.

Initially, Alexandra was noted to be "devastated" by the realization that she had to choose between the man she'd fallen in love with and the religion she'd grown up believing. After some time, she agreed to convert to Orthodox Christianity with the reasoning that it wasn't the same as converting to a new religion altogether and that, even as an Orthodox Christian instead of a Lutheran Protestant, she could still practice her love for God.

Interestingly, Alexandra seemed to become devout in her new faith immediately after her conversion. She no longer showed any hesitation in practicing the Russian Orthodox faith that she had once been so hesitant to embrace fully.

As is the tradition in Orthodox Christianity, Alexandra adopted the practice of worshiping religious symbols and idols—a practice that wasn't as strong in Lutheran Protestant churches. The future tsarina also showed a sudden and vigorous interest in connecting with mystics and holy men, even though some of these men only had loose claims to their divine or supernatural gifts when compared to others.

This interest would particularly affect her and her future husband's places on the throne when she would later become close to one holy man in particular. While he was a lesser-known Russian monk when she first met him, most historians today recognize him as the interesting and infamous figure he became later on. That man was Grigori Yefimovich Rasputin.

For now, though, the German princess's conversion from Lutheran Protestantism to Russian Orthodox Christianity cleared the path for her marriage to Nicholas. After all, she could now rule by his side as not only the head of Russia but also as the head of the Russian Orthodox Church. By converting, she would also rid speculations of whether or not Nicholas was loyal to the Russian Orthodox Church. Her decision to convert paved the way for the approval of their marriage from both officials and the Russian populace alike.

Yet, the couple still wouldn't marry right away. Their wedding wouldn't occur until after the death of Tsar Alexander III, which wasn't far off on the horizon.

Chapter 2 – The Last Tsar's Rise to Power

Up until his father's death, Nicholas had one major job. He was to live his life in a nondescript way so he wouldn't draw the attention of rumors before he took the throne. His mother, Maria, worried that in his youthful exuberance he would forget his duties, once wrote to him:

> Never forget that everyone's eyes are turned on you now, waiting to see what your first independent steps in life will be. Always be polite and courteous with everybody so that you get along with all your comrades without discrimination, although without too much familiarity or intimacy, and never listen to flatterers.

Despite the fact that Nicholas often wrote of a life full of late nights with excessive drinking, he quickly wrote his mother back, dutifully answering, "I will always try to follow your advice, my dearest darling Mama. One has to be cautious with everybody at the start."

However, at the time, both Nicholas and his family were under the impression that he would hold the role of tsarevich for quite some time. After all, despite some health issues, his father was still young and was expected to live another thirty or so years.

Unfortunately, this wasn't the case. Due to a fatal kidney disease known as nephritis, Tsar Alexander III's reign came to an end with his death on November 1st, 1894. Now, the throne and the fate of Russia were left to his son, and Nicholas took on the full title of Tsar Nicholas II. As he lacked the proper training, which was compounded by the unexpected timeline, Nicholas was left unprepared to rule.

While this was a matter of avoidance for Alexander III, the results of his choices were something neither Nicholas nor Russia could ignore once he took the throne. Generally, all Nicholas knew as tsar was that he was unprepared for the position and that he held a genuine disdain for the way his father had led the country: under an iron fist with cruel policies. Not long after the death of his father, but before the coronation that would make him the tsar of Russia, Nicholas confided in one of his cousins, saying, "What am I going to do? What is going to happen to me, to all of Russia? I am not prepared to be Tsar. I never wanted to become one. I know nothing of the business of ruling."

Yet, despite his own admission of being woefully underprepared, Nicholas was destined to take the throne all the same. Luckily, he did have someone who had a knack for ruling in his corner: his bride-to-be, the future Tsarina Alexandra. She supported Nicholas during his first acts as the ruler of Russia. This included standing by his side through his father's funeral. On November 26th, 1894, the couple finally wed in a ceremony held at the Winter Palace.

Unfortunately, this first step taken by the new tsar and empress failed to take one major concept into consideration: the intense superstition of the Russian people during this era. Tsarina Alexandra was quickly labeled the "funeral bride" because of the close proximity between the death of Alexander III and the new rulers' wedding. Many people in Russia saw this act as an omen of future struggles that Russia would have to endure under their rule. In fact, it was this start on the wrong foot that would first sow distrust between the tsarina and her new people.

Another factor that weighed on the new couple was Alexandra's general distaste for traditional royal life. The new empress didn't follow old traditions well, such as her failure to smile on command. While today this might seem like a small detail, the tsarina's stoic facial expressions were often read by her subjects as a sign of an aloof and uncaring personality. However, Alexandra deeply cared about the Russian people; she just failed to show it in traditional terms, which was something that both she and her husband struggled with throughout their reign.

Alexandra also wasn't a fan of the royal court and living in the midst of St. Petersburg. Because of this, she convinced Nicholas to move away into a new home in the countryside, situated about fifteen miles outside of St. Petersburg. Eager to please his wife and still disillusioned by the life of a tsar, Nicholas agreed, and the family relocated.

Their countryside estate was a palace in its own right. Rather than completely stepping out of the luxury of the palace, the tsar and tsarina simply chose more luxurious trappings in a rural setting. Their new home was still outfitted with fantastic gardens, carefully manicured natural surroundings, and sprawling rooms for the family to enjoy.

The disadvantage of moving out of St. Petersburg was that the new rulers were no longer in the epicenter of Russia, where most political decisions were made and where the remainder of the governing authority of Russia resided. Nicholas, who still didn't show much of an interest in his role as tsar, was happy to rely on intermediaries to rule by proxy from his rural estate.

This lack of interest in ruling the country was partly due to the fact that Alexander III had never taught Nicholas how to run the government. Floundering on his own, Nicholas leaned heavily on his advisors, many of whom had obtained their employment while his father was in charge. Thus, despite the fact that Nicholas had recoiled from the strict policies of his father, he was still allowing many of the same authority figures from Alexander III's era to remain in power in his cabinet, guiding him through many of his decisions.

By moving out of St. Petersburg, the tsar sent another message to his people and, in a way, made the same mistakes as his father. Just as Alexander III saw his father as a weak ruler and moved toward a heavy-handed, more authoritarian rule, Nicholas went in the extreme opposite direction of his father as well. Instead of harkening back to the more liberal policies of his grandfather, though, Nicholas chose to step back altogether, taking on a more hands-off approach. Looking back on his rule, many historians have noted that one of the many decisions that led to the downfall of Nicholas was that while he wasn't considered quite as tyrannical as his father, he often came across as a distant leader. This was something that didn't aid the unrest in Russia at the time, as the people were hoping for active change. Instead, as tsar, Nicholas primarily offered inaction in the early days of his rule.

By 1895, the couple was heavily focused on the expansion of their family, and they even welcomed their first child into the world on November 16ᵗʰ, 1895. Like many monarchs, the two were hopeful that their child would be a boy since they would then have a viable heir to the Russian throne. When the child was born, though, the two greeted a baby girl, Grand Duchess Olga. Despite their hopefulness for an heir, the couple greeted their daughter with joy. In a journal kept by Tsar Nicholas II, he noted the birth of his daughter, writing, "God, what happiness! I can hardly believe it's really our child!"

Another unique thing the couple did was attend to their child personally. Many royal families relied on intricate networks of nannies and staff members. Some of the staff later recalled being surprised to see the tsar and tsarina frequently take time out of their busy days just to spend time with their daughter and other future children.

This brought up another issue in Nicholas's distance from his people, however. While he was already loath to involve himself in heavy political matters, he now had the added weight of making time for his daughter and eventually other children. This got to the point that the tsar was hesitant to take time away from his family, even if Russia was calling on him in the case of a national emergency. This only enhanced the divide between the tsar and the Russian people.

The new tsar didn't have long before his leadership skills were put to task with a tragedy. Even worse, the calamity took place during his coronation, which not only immediately reflected poorly on him but also added to the negative superstitions surrounding the royal family.

As with the tsars before him, the coronation of Tsar Nicholas II was meant to be a time of revelry and merriment. Thanks to poor planning and misinformation, the time that was usually dedicated to celebration quickly turned into a tragedy.

Coronations in Russia came with plenty of celebration. While the lower class wasn't expecting to live like kings during them, they did generally expect to eat and drink well to honor the rise of the new tsar. Expecting the average fare for a coronation, these attendees were outraged when they heard word that there was little alcohol left at the event to provide for everyone. They were so outraged, in fact, that they began to rush in tandem to get their fair share of the spoils of the revelry. The problem quickly escalated when this mad dash escalated into a full-blown riot.

During the event, wooden ramparts had been temporarily placed on the palace lawn. Some of the crowd began to trip over these, and when they did, they were quickly trampled by the rest of the incoming crowd. The more intense the crowd became, the more people fell and met their demise under their feet. At the end of the day, approximately 1,400 of the tsar's new subjects had died in the chaos.

Nicholas, still carrying the sensitive personality that he had developed in his boyhood, reacted in horror and grief when he learned of the news. So much so, in fact, that he nearly canceled the rest of the festivities and a meeting with a visiting French delegation. He was only convinced not to do this when his advisors urged him to maintain the scheduled visit because canceling would be seen as an insult to the French delegation. At the time, France was one of Russia's chief and most powerful allies, making them a crucial demographic to keep happy. To avoid any insult, the meeting was kept on the schedule, even though the new tsar was fairly appalled by what had occurred. In addition, while this may have pleased the French delegation, such tragedy striking at the tsar's coronation added to the superstitious suspicions that the Russian people held of his reign.

The new ruler did attempt to redeem himself by repairing the negative sentiments that this event had inspired in his people. He spent time visiting the families of the injured and fallen, and he made an effort to cover as much of the medical and funeral expenses that arose from the tragedy.

Tsar Nicholas did see some international political redemption for Russia when he went to the Hague Peace Conference of 1899. This conference was designed as a chance for nations to come together and develop an overarching standard for the rules of war and how war crimes should be handled. The conference would later be incarnated into organizations like the League of Nations.

In 1899, in a world before the world wars, the harshest and most brutal war that Europe had seen in recent history was the Crimean War. This war was a bloody disaster for Russia when Nicholas I, Nicholas II's great-grandfather and namesake, was in power. Much like his grandfather, Alexander II, Nicholas approached the Hague Peace Conference with an attitude of both regret and humility on the part of Russia, showing true remorse for the conflict. This was actually one of Nicholas's earliest successful moments as a leader, and it even earned him a nomination for a Nobel Peace Prize two years later in 1901. This time, the tsar had shown to the world that he had great potential as a peacetime leader.

This also highlights an interesting fact about Nicholas. Despite the fact that the new tsar often failed to grasp the intricacies of the politics within Russia, he was a strong leader when it came to foreign relations and foreign policy.

Back within the safety of the palace, Alexandra and Nicholas had another challenge facing them: the necessary production of an heir. After their first daughter, they gave birth to three more children: Tatiana, Maria, and Anastasia. While Nicholas and Alexandra showed nothing but love for their children and excitement at the prospect of expanding their family, they were starting to feel the pressure of producing an heir to the Russian throne. Without a son, they didn't have a secure follower to take over Russia when Nicholas died.

The anxiety that this situation created led the family to desperate measures. They wanted to make sure that they had a son to pass the title down to, as they were living under the assumption that, of course, the empire would continue for generations after their deaths.

This concern for a son led to some drastic measures, especially from the tsarina. Alexandra's fixation on surrounding herself with holy figures, including mystics and those claiming to be divine, only strengthened during this time period, as she was truly desperate for help. The family became particularly close to Nizer Anthelme Philippe. Philippe was a mystic who practiced beliefs that were loosely based on the practices of Russian Orthodoxy. He swore to Tsarina Alexandra that she would give birth to a boy.

On August 12th, 1904, the family's wish came true, and the tsarina gave birth to a boy named Alexei Nikolaevich. This helped to confirm Alexandra's belief in the mystics, and she would continue to surround herself with them as the years passed.

However, their joy wouldn't last. When Alexei was young, the Romanovs noticed something about him. He would easily get hurt and bleed profusely. Before long, the royal family had an answer, as little Alexei was diagnosed with hemophilia, a blood disorder Alexandra had as well. To put it simply, Alexei's blood struggled to clot, which allowed the blood to keep flowing. This put the Russian heir at great risk because even a minor injury could prove fatally dangerous.

The family was scared for their son, and the tsarina was particularly hard on herself. Her brother had died from complications with hemophilia when he was young, and she blamed herself for his medical condition. It didn't help that women were known to be carriers of hemophilia. This means that for Alexei to have hemophilia, the genetic sequence for it was passed down through Alexandra, not Nicholas. Of course, his likelihood of the disease was also increased by the amount of inbreeding amongst monarchs in Europe at the time. Even Alexandra and Nicholas were related through several different lineages.

Alexandra quickly came to the conclusion that it was her lack of faith that had led her family to hardship. She doubled her efforts as a Christian and spent more time praying and surrounding herself with the divine. This would lead the ruling family toward one mystic who would become a central character in the reign of the final tsar: a man named Rasputin.

In fact, the illness that haunted baby Alexei and his mother would prove to cast quite a shadow on the Romanovs. Pierre Gilliard, a tutor to Tsarevich Alexei and his sisters, would later state:

> The illness of the Tsarevich cast its shadow over the whole of the concluding period of Tsar Nicholas II's reign and alone can explain it. Without appearing to be, it was one of the main causes of his fall, for it made possible the phenomenon of Rasputin and resulted in the fatal isolation of the sovereigns who lived in a world apart, wholly absorbed in the tragic anxiety which had to be concealed from all eyes.

Once again, it's crucial to note that Nicholas and Alexandra had a unique view compared to other royals at the time. These children, Alexei included, were not simply carriers of the Romanov name but were also deeply loved by their parents. The anxiety that the couple held was not just over the thought of losing an heir but also the fear of losing a child they deeply loved.

In the meantime, Nicholas and Alexandra made sure that their son and heir was carefully monitored. He wasn't allowed to play like the other children his age, and he lived a rather coddled lifestyle, as his parents feared for his safety. For Alexei, simply tripping over an object or getting a small cut could prove fatal. Nicholas assigned caretakers to his son, who gained the nickname "sailor nannies" for having the strength of a sailor. These caregivers were to watch Alexei at all times and make sure no harm came to him. If he looked like he was going to fall, his caretakers were there to catch him before he hit the ground.

As for Nicholas, he finally had a handle on the deep anxiety and concern of producing an heir only to realize that his son's life was easily threatened. In time, Nicholas shared that it was his belief in God that pushed him and his family through. He believed that if God gave his family this challenge, it wasn't his place to question it or wish otherwise. Rather, he had to face it with dignity and faith.

Chapter 3 – The Russo-Japanese War and the Massacre of Bloody Sunday

In 1904, Tsar Nicholas II would have to do more than appear humble at the gatherings of world leaders and prove his worth as a peacetime figurehead. Now, his leadership skills were put to the test through the first acts of the Russo-Japanese War, which would last from 1904 to 1905.

Despite the short length of the Russo-Japanese War, the actions that were taken during it were crucial for a few different reasons. For one, it served as a reflection of how Nicholas would perform in holding Russia's position as a world superpower, both in how he reacted to threats and held onto Russian territories against another powerful country.

In addition, the Russo-Japanese War showed some of the major issues that would come to play in World War I and the later World War II. This has earned it the unofficial nickname "World War Zero" from historians. As for Nicholas II, this would serve as the first test of his skills as a military leader.

By 1904, Russia was a growing empire. One of their important strongholds was a shipping center in Vladivostok, Siberia. This port wasn't open all through the year, though, so Russia was in need of another port in the Pacific Ocean to utilize during the warmer months of the year. At the time, Nicholas was particularly interested in the Korean Peninsula and the Liaodong Peninsula, which resided in what is now modern-day China.

However, this expansion wasn't set on a paved route. Another strong Asian power at the time, Japan, wasn't ready to let Russia's expansion continue unchecked. Their concern about Russian influence in Asia had only grown since the First Sino-Japanese War in 1895. At first, they tried to negotiate with the tsar and his generals by agreeing to cede Manchuria to Russia in order to keep the Japanese influence over Korea strong. However, the tsar declined this offer and demanded that the area of Korea, which was, at the time, a large, undivided country, which lay north of the 39th parallel, be neutral ground rather than under Japanese control.

Unhappy with the deal, Japan not only rescinded its offer but also launched a preemptive attack on Russia on February 8th, 1904, once the negotiations started to break down. The Japanese forces attacked the Russian Far East Fleet, which was caught off guard, placing them at an immediate disadvantage in the battle. To make up for this lack of preparedness, Nicholas ordered the Baltic Fleet to move into position immediately to help the Far East Fleet, but it was a long journey from the Baltic to where the Far East Fleet was positioned in Manchuria. To reach them, the Baltic Fleet was forced to go around the southern tip of South Africa and between Korea and Japan through the Tsushima Strait.

As a result of this lengthy journey, the order was ultimately ineffective. During Japanese Admiral Tōgō Heihachirō's attack, about two-thirds of Russia's navy sank to the bottom of the sea, and the war as a whole would claim about 6,000 Russian lives.

The war finally ended with the Treaty of Portsmouth, which was mediated by US President Theodore Roosevelt in Kittery, Maine, at the Portsmouth Naval Shipyard. Baron Komura Jutarō represented Japan, while Nicholas sent Sergei Witte, a minister in his government, on behalf of Russia. During the talks and in media coverage, the blame of the majority of the casualties was assigned to Russia due to its brutal tactics, which caused many civilian casualties. This was mostly due to the accusations of Russians burning and looting villages in Manchuria. In the end, the conflict was a brutal one for Russia, as it was largely seen as a strategic failure and a political humiliation.

The signing of the Treaty of Portsmouth was far from the last conflict that Nicholas would have to handle as the tsar. World War I was only years away, and the first concrete steps of the Russian Revolution were already at Nicholas's doorstep.

The Russo-Japanese War officially ended on September 5th, 1905, with the signing of the Treaty of Portsmouth. However, even before it ended, the unrest in Russia was starting to build. The war had played directly into Russia's internal tensions. To many Russians, the humiliation of their defeat wasn't worth the loss of lives. In addition, this dissatisfaction was compounded with other struggles that many Russians were facing in trying to support themselves and their families. On January 9th, 1905, St. Petersburg would be the site of an event that would go down in history as Bloody Sunday.

The uprising was led by a young but already popular priest named Father Georgy Gapon and began with more than 10,000 workers on strike. The goal of the crowd was to march directly to the palace. They genuinely believed that the tsar wasn't a flawed leader but that he was unaware of their plight.

The crowd had, by modern standards, reasonable requests, such as the implementation of an eight-hour workday and a living wage. The factory workers marched toward the palace, and the crowd would build to over 120,000 people by the time they started to arrive near their final destination. They hoisted banners for Nicholas and anyone who was curious about their cause that read, in part, "We are impoverished, we are oppressed, overburdened with excessive toil, contemptuously treated. Death is better than the prolongation of our unbearable suffering. We beseech thy help."

The crowd also held up banners with Nicholas's face on them. They sang religious hymns and "God Save the Tsar!" the religious anthem of the country at the time.

While separate marches erupted around the city, they all converged together to head toward the Winter Palace to see the tsar at around 2 p.m. As the protestors marched on, they were met with soldiers manning roadblocks toward the palace. Already determined to achieve their mission and inform the tsar of their suffering, the demonstrators attempted to make their way through the roadblocks. As the crowd began to disobey the orders of the soldiers, the tsar's armed men began to open fire on them without warning.

What had been a fairly organized and peaceful movement moments ago was now chaos. Protestors who weren't immediately gunned down were forced to flee in a panic for their lives, some leaving friends and comrades bleeding on the ground behind them.

By the time the gunfire quieted, the snow around the palace was dyed red with blood. Russian bodies lay in the snow for the crime of asking for a better, more livable existence. The official count released after the tragedy stated that ninety-two people had died on Bloody Sunday, with several hundred wounded. However, this number was probably greatly minimized, and later, revolutionaries would multiply it as high as a thousand or more. Today, it's generally believed that about 200 Russians were killed in the massacre, with many more injured.

As for the leaders of the march, they were seized after the gunfire stopped, and the blame was quickly placed on them. Those who escaped would tell horror stories of the event and were the main ones responsible for exaggerating the number of casualties. As for Father Gabon, the primary leader of the march, he escaped as well.

Perhaps what made this historical event all the more tragic is that the palace that the protestors were marching toward wasn't even housing the tsar at the moment. Nicholas was initially unaware of the demonstration and its bloody end. Instead, he was enjoying a meal with his wife and children at their countryside estate when the massacre took place.

That isn't to say that Nicholas hadn't been warned about a potential uprising. Officials at the time were expecting unrest from the populace and had warned Nicholas with their concerns. The day before Bloody Sunday, Nicholas's ministers had urged him to hasten to the palace, hoping that his presence or some potential action would limit tensions and ease the extent of the unrest. However, the tsar refused to budge on the matter. Convinced that the mere sight of the armed guards would quell the demonstrators' rebellious spirits, the tsar chose to stay with his family, out of harm's way.

While he found the event tragic, the leader was neither apologetic nor sympathetic to the victims. Nicholas failed to condemn his soldiers for firing on the crowd and inciting violence. Instead, he placed the blame solely on the protestors. He called out the crowd for provoking the gunmen and excused his soldiers' actions, claiming that they feared being overrun. The tsar even went so far as to call on the protestors to apologize for their actions, blaming their disturbance for the loss of life. On the tragedy of Bloody Sunday, he said, "Serious disorders took place in Petersburg when the workers tried to come to the Winter Palace. The troops have been forced to fire in several parts of the city and there are many killed and wounded. Lord, how painful and sad this is!"

Once again, the tsar's closest confidant and highest advisor, his wife Alexandra, didn't paint him in a bad light either. True to form, she blamed the protestors and those around her husband. In writing to her sister, Princess Victoria of Battenberg, she said the following:

> You understand the crisis we are going through! It is a time full of trials indeed. My poor Nicky's cross is a heavy one to

bear, all the more as he has nobody on whom he can thoroughly rely and who can be a real help to him...Don't believe all the horrors the foreign papers say. They make one's hair stand on end—foul exaggeration. Yes, the troops, alas, were obliged to fire. Repeatedly the crowd was told to retreat and that Nicky was not in town...and that one would be forced to shoot, but they would not heed and so blood was shed.

The tsarina continued, recounting the narrative that Nicholas and his government were pushing. Since her relationship with Nicholas was close, the empress would have an active hand in ruling Russia during the final Romanov reign. She also believed that, in this case, as well as many others, her husband and his men were irrevocably in the right. As such, her influence didn't come in the people's favor. She even continued in her letter to say, "All over the country, of course, it is spreading. The Petition had only two questions concerning the workmen and all the rest was atrocious: separation of the Church from the Government, etc. etc. Had a small deputation brought, calmly, a real petition for the workmen's good, all would have been otherwise."

Although Alexandra was on Nicholas's side, there were many who were not, and some influential people contacted Nicholas and tried to sway him. The writer Leo Tolstoy would later advise the tsar in reference to Bloody Sunday and his actions thereafter, saying, "I do not want to die without having told you what great evil you will bring to yourself and to millions if you continue on your present course." The words of the Russian writer fell on deaf ears, though.

Nicholas's actions had eroded one of the most telling barriers between the suffering Russians and the Russian Revolution. Rather than being seen as the Father of Russia and the "Holy Father," the tsar now held nicknames such as "Bloody Nicholas" and "The People's Executioner." Later, one of the protestors present at the Bloody

Sunday massacre would insist, "There is no God any longer. There is no Tsar!"

Father Gapon also released a statement on the event from his place in hiding. He denounced the tsar, saying,

> Nicholas Romanov, formerly Tsar and at present soul-murderer of the Russian empire. The innocent blood of workers, their wives and children lies forever between you and the Russian people...May all the blood which must be spilled fall upon you, Hangman! I call upon all the socialist parties of Russia to come to an immediate agreement among themselves and begin an armed uprising against Tsarism.

However, Father Gapon wasn't as well listened to as later revolutionary leaders. The leaders within the Socialist Revolutionary Party held disdain for him due to his supposed ties with the police force. Father Gapon was later sentenced to death and was found dead in Finland in an abandoned cottage in 1906.

After Bloody Sunday, the tsar was advised to distance himself from the event and reduce his role in it as much as possible; however, he ignored these orders. He even held an event to receive a delegation of thirty-four workers at Tsarskoe Selo, who were handpicked to meet him. They were given tea, but rather than being allowed to share ideas, they were lectured by the tsar like children. Nicholas told them that they needed to follow two principles. They should both support and respect his soldiers in the field, and they should ignore revolutionaries, referring to their advice as wicked and treacherous. When this delegation of workers returned to St. Petersburg, they were laughed at, ignored, or assaulted rather than received as the careful messengers of the tsar.

In one fell swoop, Nicholas's actions not only condemned him, but it also eroded the general populace's trust and belief in the position and title of the tsar. Russia was now primed like never before for a revolution.

And it didn't take long for this fact to be proven either. Bloody Sunday was only the beginning of revolutionary action. Less than a month later, Nicholas's uncle was assassinated outside of their Kremlin apartment. Much like Nicholas's grandfather, Alexander II, Grand Duke Sergei Alexandrovich was killed when a revolutionary threw a bomb at him as he stepped out of his carriage. His wife, Alexandra's older sister, ran to her husband but found nothing left of him after the bomb blast.

The grand duke's assassination was caused not only by his hatred of revolutionaries but also his combativeness to reform and his pride. When the grand duchess visited her husband's assassin, Ivan Kalayev, in prison, she offered to plead for his life. In return, all he had to do was ask the tsar for a pardon. Yet Kalayev refused. He simply told the widow that his death would serve to aid the cause of the Socialist Revolutionary Party. The change they were fighting for was no longer just simple reform; they wanted the autocracy of the tsarism completely overthrown and replaced.

1905 was a time of building unrest in Russia. By the time mid-October rolled around, a building strike had taken full force. It went from a small, more segmented movement to a full strike that seized Russia from the Urals to Warsaw. It disrupted train schedules, closed schools and hospitals, shut down newspapers and factories, and caused the delivery of food to cease. This left Russia in a state of disarray, and many citizens were left starving and desperate. In the cities, crowds would chant and march, while at private residences, red flags were flown from the rooftops. Farther out in the countryside, estates were raided by peasants, and manor houses were often burned down in anger and protest.

This culminated in the creation of a new workers' organization known as a soviet, or, in more English terms, a council. It seemingly came from nothing, much like the marches and strikes that bore little foreshadowing to what was to come. It was led by Leon Trotsky, who was a part of the Menshevik branch of the Marxist Social Democratic

Labour Party. He was also a talented orator who could easily whip dissatisfied workers into a frenzy of action.

This ultimately led to one of the first concrete but unsuccessful steps of reform: the creation of a duma, or a representative council. When asked on whether he should crush the rebellion with force or focus on reform, Nicholas wrote to his mother, saying:

> The other way out would be to give the people their civil rights, freedom of speech and press, also to have all laws confirmed by a state Duma—that, of course, would be a constitution. [Sergei] Witte defends this energetically. He says that, while it is not without risk, it is the only way out at the present moment. Almost everybody I had an opportunity of consulting is of the same opinion. Witte put it to me quite clearly that he would accept the Presidency of the Council of Ministers only on condition that his program was agreed to and his action not interfered with. He...drew up the Manifesto. We discussed it for two days and in the end, invoking God's help, I signed it...My only consolation is that such is the will of God and this grave decision will lead my Russia out of the intolerable chaos she has been in for nearly a year.

Chapter 4 – Nicholas's Reforms and the Introduction of Rasputin

While Nicholas did agree to the creation of a duma, that didn't mean he was a great and willing reformer in the early 20th century. The tsar looked out at his suffering people and saw not that they need governmental change but rather that their faith in God was weakening. He looked at the conditions that his people lived in and the woes they carried, and he blamed it on a lack of piety and missing societal discipline.

This makes some sense, though. After all, the Russian people and Nicholas himself had been taught that the tsarism was inextricably linked to religiosity. Not only was the tsar, to an extent, a religious leader, but the title of the tsar was also a birthright; therefore, it was a title chosen by God. Thus, once the Russian masses, who were protesting in the streets of the cities, burning manors in the countryside, and even waving red flags in their own homes, started to denounce the tsar, much of their opposition saw it as a denouncement of both the Russian Orthodoxy and of God Himself.

As tsar, Nicholas's line of thinking basically harkened back to the extremism that he once questioned in his father and even the authoritarianism that the people in his life had encouraged from his time as a pupil. Instead of automatically considering reform, Nicholas wondered if a firmer hand would help guide his people back into a more peaceful society.

In the end, as would prove to be the case quite often, Nicholas's decisions would be fueled by his desire and duty to preserve Russia as an empire rather than his desire to answer his people's demands.

On October 30th, 1905, Nicholas would sign a manifesto that he wrote with Witte. This would come to be known as the Imperial Manifesto or the October Manifesto, and it would establish the duma the people had been asking for. This would provide Russia with a semi-constitutional monarchy, which was a large step from the absolute power of the monarchal autocracy it was before. The Imperial Manifesto promised Russians that they would possess the "freedom of conscience, speech, assembly, and association." The manifesto also stated, "No law may go into force without the consent of the Duma."

This was a significant step for the Russian revolutionaries, but it wasn't a total step either. The Duma offered representation in their government, but it didn't give nearly as much power to the public as the British Parliament did, and it was a far cry from democracies like the one held in the United States.

It was also a step that took drastic measures to encourage the tsar to take action. Perhaps among the most dramatic was the military, which was struggling to combat the threat of societal and governmental collapse. Also, Nicholas's cousin, a commander in the St. Petersburg Military District, resorted to violent threats. He bypassed peaceful communication and barged into the tsar's private quarters, brandishing a weapon. Rather than an assassination attempt, he put the gun to his own head and threatened suicide if Nicholas wouldn't consider the needs of his people and the actions that would maintain peace in Russia. It was at this point that Nicholas finally caved into demands and truly considered the Imperial Manifesto.

There were still areas where the tsar held almost total power, such as foreign policy, and he also held absolute power over the hiring and firing of ministers. In other words, the Duma was primarily focused on laws within Russia—the ones that would most directly affect the Russian people and their livelihoods. The Duma is also highly praised by historians for its ability to reach important benchmarks in their government that other countries—specifically those in Western Europe—would take years or even centuries to reach.

Yet the situation in Russia failed to improve. The people's dissatisfaction didn't even remain stagnant; rather, it continued to worsen. This was partially thanks to the attitude of Nicholas, who would frequently feign agreement with the Duma only to turn back on his word later when it came time for him to make a decision. He once said about the new arm of his government that "The Duma is such filth...a hearth of revolutionaries."

Political divides also placed Witte in the middle of disagreements. From the right, he received sentiments of disdain or even outright hatred for his role in degrading the absolute power of the monarchy, while the political left failed to trust him thanks to his close relationship with the tsar. At one point, a liberal Russian historian named Paul Miliukov would say of the period, "Nothing has changed, the struggle goes on."

One of the largest forces against the Imperial Manifesto was a group known as the Black Hundred. Once the Imperial Manifesto was passed, most of the population with revolutionary leanings were overjoyed. They quickly took to the streets to test the extent of their new powers by expressing their views. At first, it seemed like a miracle had taken place in Russia, as individuals were free to speak their minds no matter if they were criticizing or supporting the laws and policies that the tsar had in mind. They were even able to criticize the tsar as a person or as a leader. These were all things that used to be prohibited, with grave consequences for those caught doing it.

While the Russian police force and soldiers, for the most part, respected these new freedoms, the Black Hundred did not. They were diehard loyalists to the tsar and took on the role of an unofficial paramilitary on the tsar's behalf, often clashing directly with the more liberal protesters. The abuse they hurled ranged from verbal altercations to physical abuse. If a person shared too many opinions against the tsar or held what could be considered too much of a revolutionary viewpoint at the time, the Black Hundred wouldn't hesitate to do everything in their power to silence them.

While the support of this group didn't officially come from the Russian government, Nicholas did what he could to unofficially show his favor. One of the best examples is when he ordered his police force to stand down when the Black Hundred started to berate or even physically assault Russians who used their newfound rights to dissent against the tsar. These protestors quickly learned that if the nationalist pro-tsar group showed up, they could expect no help from the authorities who were officially instated to protect them and their rights.

At the same time, the royal family's loss of power had a deep impact on Nicholas and Alexandra, who were both raised with the idea that rulers wielded absolute power, as it was their birthright. The support that they used to receive from their people faded once actions like those taken on Bloody Sunday separated the tsar from his previously perceived position of being incapable of wrongdoing.

As such, it was no surprise when the two leaders started to question themselves. For the first time in Nicholas's life, the Russian people weren't looking at him as God's gift or as the protector of Russia. Now, he was faced with crowds that were quick to highlight his flaws and call for him to fix them or, in the more extreme sects of the revolution, to step down altogether.

As the deeply religious couple was prone to do, they started to look to God for answers. Thanks to Alexandra's developed faith in proclaimed holy men, she brought another one into their life. On

November 1ˢᵗ, 1905, Tsar Nicholas II and Tsarina Alexandra would meet a man that would shape their lives more than they could possibly know, a holy man named Rasputin.

Rasputin claimed that he was a prophet and a healer, and it was the healer aspect that made him the most interesting to Nicholas and Alexandra. This is because while turmoil ripped through Russia, there was turmoil within the royal family as well. Tsarevich Alexei's health had worsened to the point that there were several instances where the young boy was so close to death that he was given his last rites, with the family being encouraged to say their goodbyes.

However, seemingly only by miraculous powers, Rasputin was able to come to Alexei's bedside and pluck him from the brink of death, putting him back on his feet again.

At the time, Rasputin seemed like the holy man they'd been looking for—a true mystic with the power to reverse imminent death itself. Yet, in the modern day, historians don't quite believe in the magic that Rasputin wielded. Instead, the more commonly held belief by historians is that Rasputin likely healed Alexei by altering his treatment plan. The tsarevich likely received aspirin as a part of his treatment, which, in today's standards, is an unwise treatment for hemophilia because it's a blood thinner. As such, it would have made the already anemic boy bleed even more, and with a condition like hemophilia, this could be deadly.

Rasputin's miracle cure probably included telling his doctors not to give him aspirin, which would, of course, quickly improve his condition. From Nicholas's and Alexandra's perspective, though, they watched a holy man walk into their son's room, say a brief prayer with him, and then promise him that he will be all right. Like many religious leaders, his performative nature lent to his stature as a holy man.

To Nicholas and Alexandra, though, it didn't matter how or why Rasputin did what he did. In the end, he saved their son's life. Because of this fact, the family trusted him so much that he quickly became a staple in their court and even one of Nicholas's most trusted advisors.

Unfortunately, Rasputin also brought scandal to Nicholas's court in a time when Nicholas should have avoided scandal at all costs. Rasputin was well known for drinking often, frequenting brothels, and being quite the womanizer. This all contrasted greatly with his proclaimed image as a holy man. In fact, for most of the people of this deeply religious country, this was seen as an unforgivable sacrilege.

As such a controversial figure, Rasputin's life was also a breeding ground for rumors and gossip. It wasn't long after he started to spend time in the court that Russians would start to whisper of the holy man's womanizing. Rumors even began to circulate that he'd taken on the tsarina as a lover.

Even more detrimental, many Russians believed that Rasputin was using the tsar since he had become Nicholas's advisor and was becoming the true ruler. There were a few consequences of this. For one, it gave the Russians and Nicholas a scapegoat when poor actions were taken, although Nicholas genuinely appreciated Rasputin, so he most likely would never place undue blame on him. On the other hand, the thought that Rasputin was using the tsar and tsarina furthered the narrative that Nicholas was a weak leader. It was a rumor that both took the blame off of the tsar and made him seem like the butt of the joke, as he wasn't wise enough to see when an obviously false prophet was taking advantage of him.

One of Rasputin's early critics was the leader of the Duma, elected Prime Minister Pyotr Stolypin. He even went so far as to launch an underground investigation into Rasputin's life. This focused on his activities, his reputation as a holy man, and his potential goals in being so close to the tsar. By the conclusion of his investigation, he fought for Rasputin to be removed from the tsar's court. During this period, Rasputin split his time between the company of the royal family and his own family and was frequently known to travel home to Siberia.

When he was absent from the court, it was easier for Stolypin to make his case and try to bar the holy man from returning.

This wasn't something that Nicholas and Alexandra took well. Not only were the two once again angered by an outside influence on their lives and how they exerted their power, but they were also genuinely concerned that without the influence of Rasputin, their son would die from his condition.

Before Stolypin's investigation could result in concrete action, he would be cut down by an assassin. On September 18th, 1911, Stolypin would attend a production of *The Tale of Tsar Saltan*, which Tsar Nicholas attended as well. Stolypin's bodyguards left the prime minister alone for only enough time to step outside to smoke a cigarette when the assassin, a self-proclaimed leftwing activist named Dmitry Bogrov, ran up to Stolypin and opened fire. As he was being attacked, Stolypin tried to get the tsar's attention, as Nicholas sat in the overhead imperial box. When the assassin fled, he desperately tried to catch the tsar's eye by waving his arms frantically over his head. In the end, the tsar remained unharmed, likely saved by his bodyguards reacting to the sound of gunfire, even if Stolypin failed to catch Nicholas's eye. Stolypin only lived for three more days before he succumbed to his wounds.

The assassin was quickly apprehended, and he was executed for his crimes only ten days after the shooting—about a week after Stolypin's demise. During this time, Nicholas took the chance to reinstate Rasputin into his court now that his loudest critic was no longer in the way.

This served as a breeding ground for conspiracy theories. Nicholas didn't help the suspicions of the Russians either when he denied an investigation into the assassination of Stolypin around the same time he reinstated Rasputin. This added suspicion only furthered the divide between Nicholas and the Russian people, who were beginning to think more and more that the tsar was flawed and perhaps not to be trusted.

Further solidifying his reentry into the court, Rasputin was available just when Alexei seemed to need him the most. The family was on vacation to Poland when Alexei injured himself, and what would be a slight inconvenience to most quickly turned fatal for the poor boy. The doctors vacationing with them and those in Poland were sure that the tsarevich was going to die, and the boy was even given the last rites for the dying by Russian Orthodox values. In a desperate final plea, Alexandra and Nicholas called Rasputin, begging him to save their son's life. Rasputin answered them, "God had seen your tears and heard your prayers. Do not grieve. The little one will not die."

Almost immediately, Alexei seemed to heal, and he returned from the brink of death. Because of this, Nicholas and Alexandra became inextricably appreciative of and linked to Rasputin. They would continue to rely on the holy man until his eventual death.

This happened in October 1912, right on the heels of an important milestone for Nicholas, for the year 1913 marked the 300-year anniversary of the Romanov dynasty taking power. This was planned as a huge holiday. The tsar closed factories, and the masses were meant to be on the receiving end of gifts; amnesty was even granted to some of Nicholas's subjects.

Nicholas and his advisors saw this as a chance to repair the broken relationship between the tsar and his people. He hoped to use this holiday to mend bridges and eventually regain power in the long run.

On the day of the celebration, Nicholas rode a caravan through the streets of St. Petersburg, starting at the St. Petersburg Cathedral. Much to his disappointment, the day only served to highlight the weak relationship between the tsar and the masses. As he made his way through the streets, the people who watched the procession were almost completely made up of police officers who were positioned to protect the tsar from the expected crowds.

Thus, the 300th anniversary of the Romanovs' time in power was almost completely uneventful. Rather than a chance to rekindle faith in the tsar, the day was a painful reminder to Nicholas that his people no longer looked at him as their powerful and absolute ruler.

Chapter 5 – Nicholas II and the Onset of the Great War

While unrest and discontent were rising in Russia, Nicholas would soon have another crisis to worry about. When the failed celebrations for the 300th year of the Romanov reign came to an end, the world was closing in on the largest military conflict to date: the Great War, which would later come to be known as World War I.

The war started on June 28th, 1914, with the assassination of Archduke Franz Ferdinand of Austria-Hungary. While in Sarajevo, the archduke and his wife Sophie were shot by a Serbian assassin named Gavrilo Princip. The war would begin with the two countries involved in the assassination, Austria-Hungary and Serbia. Instead of simply starting and stopping with two people, Austria-Hungary and Serbia would drag all of Europe into the war. At the time, there were many tangled alliances, with countries pledging to help each other in times of war. And that time had finally come.

At the beginning of the war, Nicholas wasn't sure where Russia belonged. Years earlier, a treaty solidified Russia and Serbia as allies, and as such, Russia was naturally opted to back Serbia in the war. This was also backed by the similarities between the two countries. After all, Russia and Serbia held extensive likenesses in their cultural and ethnic identities.

The challenge to this was the threat of a declaration of war by Germany if Russia supported Serbia in any way. Since Austria-Hungary was allied with Germany, Germany was quick to follow and support their ally.

However, Serbia wasn't the only ally that Russia had. Nicholas had also forged allies with France and England, both of which would also be drawn into the war thanks to their entanglement. As these knots between countries became tighter, Europe broke out into a war that, rather than affecting a couple of countries at once, would pull all their allies into the fray and create a never-before-seen conflict that would snowball into the First World War. Russia would officially join the conflict in August 1914, after around two months since the conflict started.

On July 28th, 1914, Austria-Hungary declared war and started to attack Serbia. They dropped bombs on the Serbian capital city of Belgrade, which, in turn, pushed Russia to act because of their alliance.

When it came to Nicholas's personal views on the war, he was torn as to how Russia should intervene or if they should even intervene at all. On the one hand, the tsar and his wife were completely unprepared for a war of this scale—as was every other country in Europe. In Nicholas's case, it held the potential to strike at the heart of an already unstable climate in Russia.

On the other hand, war has set a historical precedent for drawing a country together in tough times. It held the potential to boost patriotism in the country and perhaps even heal the wounds that divided Russia. Yet there was also a chance that this concept would backfire the same way that the Russo-Japanese War had played a heavy hand in pulling the country apart.

Despite these grappling views, Nicholas still tried to avoid conflict by striking a deal with Kaiser Wilhelm II of Germany, who was his biological third cousin. Unfortunately, despite their familial bond to Queen Victoria, who was Wilhelm's grandmother and Nicholas's grandmother-in-law, the two didn't possess a strong or close relationship. Queen Victoria herself once warned Nicholas to be careful with his cousin, quoting his "mischievous and straightforward proceedings." Victoria also described the Kaiser to her own prime minister as "a hot-headed, conceited, and wrong-headed young man," which was at odds with Wilhelm's frequent claim that he was Victoria's favorite grandson. Even Nicholas once exclaimed after meeting him that the Kaiser was "raving mad!"

In the hopes of avoiding a war between their respective nations, Nicholas sent Wilhelm a telegraph on July 29th, 1914. In the telegraphs they exchanged, Nicholas started with a desperate and genuine plea. "In this serious moment, I appeal to you to help me. An ignoble war has been declared to a weak country. The indignation in Russia shared fully by me is enormous. I foresee that very soon I shall be overwhelmed by the pressure forced upon me and be forced to take extreme measures which will lead to war."

The Kaiser was quick to reply to the tsar, but his message was less promising than Nicholas had hoped for. It read:

> I...share your wish that peace should be maintained but...I cannot consider Austria's action against Serbia an "ignoble" war. Austria knows by experience that Serbian promises on paper are wholly unreliable. I understand its action must be judged as trending to get full guarantee that the Serbian promises shall become real facts. I, therefore, suggest that it would be quite possible for Russia to remain a spectator of the Austro-Serbian conflict without involving Europe in the most horrible war she ever witnessed.

The two leaders continued to send telegrams back and forth for days after that, all the time discussing the impending chaos Europe was poised to descend into. During this exchange of letters, both countries were mobilizing for war, each preparing to jump to the defense of their respective allies. Near the end of their communications, Wilhelm offered Nicholas a deal. "I have gone to the utmost limits...in my efforts to save peace...even now, you can still save the peace of Europe by stopping your military measures."

However, halting the military measures that Russia was taking wasn't such an easy choice for Nicholas. He was bound by a treaty to act as an ally to Serbia, and he informed the Kaiser of this. "It is technically impossible to stop our military preparations which were obligatory owing to Austria's mobilization. We are far from wishing for war. As long as the negotiations with Austria on Serbia's account are taking place my troops shall not make any provocative action. I give you my solemn word for this."

Sadly, Nicholas's promises and pleas were too little too late. During the time that they spoke, Wilhelm had contacted Emperor Franz Josef of Austria-Hungary for information and mediation. Josef declined and stated that Austria-Hungary was already marching on Serbia and that Russian troops were already mobilized. In turn, Wilhelm gave Nicholas an ultimatum to answer: if he wanted peace, he had twelve hours to halt the mobilization of Russian forces, or Germany would mobilize its own army. However, if Nicholas were to pull his troops back, it would fall back on Russia as a sign of an embarrassing defeat before the war even started. This would go over extremely unwell after the political embarrassment of Russia's defeat in the Russo-Japanese War.

When four o'clock on August 1ˢᵗ rolled around, the Kaiser hadn't heard back from the Russian tsar, and true to his word, he started to mobilize the German forces with the help of General Erich von Falkenhayn and Chancellor Theobald von Bethmann-Hollweg. He sent one final telegram to the tsar and then declared war on Russia.

The failed negotiations between Russia and Germany would later earn the moniker of the "Willy-Nicky Telegrams." They marked the entrance of Germany and Russia, one of the world's largest superpowers at the time, into World War I, the brutal and bloody "war to end all wars."

Within Russia, the Great War didn't have the patriotic effect that Nicholas wanted. A large part of this was because while Russia was a major superpower, partially thanks to its large army, Nicholas couldn't match the sheer number of soldiers in the army with an equal number of supplies. How it supplied that army, or rather didn't supply it, took a toll on those within Russia, both on the frontlines and at home.

The source of many people's woes was the fact that Russia's manufacturing process failed to provide for its army and its people. On the front, the infantry was largely unarmed. At the time, the army consisted of about six million Russians, but there were only four million guns available. This led to the use of ineffective tactics. For instance, at times, only part of the infantry ran into battle first, while the unarmed men hung back. As the Russian soldiers saw their comrades gunned down, they were instructed to run out into the field, grab the fallen man's gun from his body, and join the fight.

The Russian military movement was also hampered by naval movements on all sides. The German navy gained control of the Baltic Sea in the north, while the Ottoman Empire moved to close in on the Strait of the Dardanelles. With this in mind, the Russian armed forces were completely left to fight on land with no fighting chance in the naval battles. This also slowed Russian movements. As expansive as Russia was, and still is, it took a lot of time to move the large army and its supplies from place to place.

Finally, the shortage of supplies in the Russian army meant more than just a shortage of weapons to fight with. It was also increasingly difficult to feed the army adequately—a problem that bled over to the Russians back at home as well.

As they were trying to feed the troops, Nicholas's government soon found out that it had bled the national food supplies dry. This problem was only exasperated by the fact that many of the men who usually tended the fields and bolstered the food supply in Russia were now on the frontlines, making the problem much harder to address. The core of the problem quickly became clear: Russia's manufacturing output was devastatingly miscalculated. It didn't help that the onset of the Great War was dangerously close to the recovery period from the unrest that took place after the Russo-Japanese War.

The lack of food created its own problems, as most Russians could now barely afford enough bread for themselves and their families. It would inspire the chant coined by leader Vladimir Lenin, which demanded, "Peace, Land, and Bread."

During this time, Nicholas wasn't hands-on with the rebuilding process. For most meetings, he spent his time reading reports and taking notes but offered little real contribution to decisions and active discussions. He left this task to his ministers. By the time the First World War started, it was clear Russia wasn't ready for a conflict of this scale, judging by their supply chain alone.

In retaliation, Nicholas had to endure further public criticism from the war industry committees led and filled by industrialists and the people who worked for them. Instead of taking an autocratic approach this time, Nicholas opted to quietly allow these committees to exist while trying to avoid stoking the fires of rebellion. In truth, though, the tsar had little choice but to avoid conflict within Russia as much as he could. If the country fell apart from the inside, there'd be no way that Russia could hold onto the Eastern Front.

Simultaneously, in St. Petersburg, which was renamed Petrograd in 1914 to avoid the German ties to the original name, chaos was brewing as well. While Nicholas focused on the war effort, Alexandra did her best to keep him informed of internal affairs. She often warned him of the Duma, in which she identified activities that she labeled nefarious when speaking to her husband.

The Duma was partially burdened with a revolving door of prime minister appointments. At the beginning of the war, Ivan Goremykin held the position of prime minister. Unfortunately, he quickly proved that for all his experience in politics, he was an aged man. Although he stayed in office for nearly two years, he was quick to personally admit that he didn't have a grasp on modern ideals in the Russian government.

In 1916, Nicholas replaced him with a younger politician named Boris Stürmer, but he didn't last long. He was quickly replaced with Alexander Trepov, who didn't inspire much positive change either. This revolving door of officials didn't just affect the leaders at the top of the Duma. The entire Council of Ministers was constantly in a state of change, with individuals being hired and fired regularly. This added to the disarray in Petrograd and slowed progress in Russia's response to expanded crises because, after all, Nicholas still couldn't officially create Russian laws without the consent of the Duma. For that reason, he would consistently pass over officials that were said to be sympathetic to the Duma and instead appointed officials that were more sympathetic to the tsar. Unsurprisingly, this was something that was noticed by political leaders, especially those opposed to Nicholas's practices.

Finally, the tsar was able to settle on the appointment of Prince Nikolai Golitsyn, who took the position but wasn't very eager to take on the role. If Nicholas noticed that he had fewer people willing to work with him in the Russian government, he seemed oblivious to it.

At this time, the Duma criticized the tsar's moves at a near-unprecedented volume, even including the recent uprising before the First World War started. While Nicholas was carefully choosing allies that supported him, a liberal leader in the Duma named Pavel Milyukov was doing the same. Instead of doing this to retain power, though, his goal was to gain more. He wanted a cabinet that he and the other more liberal members of the Duma could choose rather than relying on Nicholas's cabinet appointments and hoping that they would serve as a fair viewpoint instead of acting as an extension of the tsar.

Even while this dispute became more heated, Nicholas didn't pay the Duma much mind. Rather, he was more focused on the front. Nicholas held a deep respect for his armed forces, a belief he held all his life. At times, he turned a blind eye to his people back at home in Russia in order to focus more on the military. He was stricken by the failures of his forces and even lamented, "I can't get to sleep at all at night when I think that the army could be starving."

The stress on Nicholas began to take a physical toll as well. He lost weight nearly to the point of emaciation and constantly sported dark bags beneath his eyes. He was frequently described as agitated and depressed, drawing concern from those close to him. Baroness Sophie Buxhoeveden was a close friend of Alexandra's, and she once posed her concerns about the tsar's health to his doctor, Eugene Botkin, worrying that his kidneys were failing him. The doctor, in equal parts, relieved and concerned her by answering that it was the tsar's heart that wasn't in order. He told her that he was administering iodine to help alleviate the stress befalling the leader but urged her to tell no one.

Throughout 1915, it seemed that the Russian army's efforts were continuously squashed. By this point, the German armies had reclaimed the Polish territory that Russia previously occupied. The Russians wouldn't see another military win until 1916 when shock troops were implemented by Russian General Alexei Brusilov to gain a victory on the Austro-Hungarian front.

Back at home, the Russians were growing tired of the continuous military failures, and Nicholas was on the hook for those mistakes. This was partially thanks to the fact that, on Rasputin's advice, Nicholas took personal and immediate control over the Russian army on August 23rd, 1915. This allowed the populace to place direct blame on the tsar for the military's failures, and it also left more leadership power to the tsarina, a woman who was even more swayed by Rasputin than the tsar.

All in all, the hope of a war reuniting the country under a banner of patriotism failed. As the fronts of World War I grew bloodier and more desperate, the tensions in Russia continued to rise, quickly moving toward a fever pitch.

Chapter 6 – The Fall of Grigori Rasputin: Russia's Scapegoat and the Romanovs' Trusted Advisor

If there was one thing that Nicholas had on his side, it was that Russia still had one scapegoat that they placed more blame on than the tsar: Rasputin. The holy man who had risen through the ranks to become one of Nicholas's most trusted advisors was a figure of suspicion to the Russian people. Not only was this man claiming to be holy, but he was also the curator of, in the court of public opinion, a debaucherous past and present. It didn't help matters that the Russian Orthodox Church had denounced Rasputin, a fact that Nicholas seemed to ignore.

Conspiracies spread like wildfire throughout Russia as to Rasputin's doings. Some whispered that Rasputin had wielded his influence to get close to the empress, whom he had taken as one of his lovers. Others thought that Rasputin's goals were far more nefarious and treasonous. This line of thinking followed the concept that Rasputin had risen through the ranks solely to grasp the tsar's ear and use his high position in Nicholas's court to wield a shady influence as Russia's secret leader.

These conspiracies would later prove to be mostly unfounded. While Rasputin did serve as one of the most trusted advisors of Nicholas and Alexandra, he wasn't a secret ruler using Nicholas as an inanimate puppet. It's also unlikely that he was having an affair with the tsarina, as there is no evidence to support such a claim. The rumor was brought about from the sexual deviancy that the Russians saw in Rasputin, as well as his influence relating to a religious sect known as the Khlyst, which believed that "sinful" behavior would actually create a stronger relationship with God rather than a more distant one.

This image wasn't helped by the fact that Rasputin's enemies did whatever was in their power to bring the so-called holy man down. This included propaganda on their behalf to smear Rasputin's already questionable name in the public eye.

At the same time, Nicholas and his wife saw little problem with Rasputin. In all likelihood, they were well aware of the growing disdain for his presence in Nicholas's court, but they either failed to recognize the severity of the situation or, more likely, put their own preferences over public opinion. Again, the tsar and tsarina saw Rasputin not only as a trusted confidante but as a healer and the only one who knew how to keep their son alive and well.

In addition, to Nicholas, Rasputin represented everything he was most interested in about his religion. While the Russian Orthodoxy disapproved and denounced Rasputin, he represented the more mythological and folkloric aspects of the religion, which Nicholas had shown an interest in from a young age.

Interestingly, many of the events that Rasputin bore the blame for weren't the actual actions that he took. For instance, he was often blamed for Russia's involvement in the Great War, but by many accounts, Rasputin had warned Nicholas that if he charged into the war, he was likely to pull Russia apart at the seams. That isn't to say

Rasputin was a revolutionary or brilliant politician, just that the blame assigned to him in many of these instances was misplaced.

Since Nicholas was determined to keep the company of Rasputin, there were individuals in Russia who concocted a plan to get rid of the supposed holy man and end his negative influence on the tsar. Interestingly, even Rasputin's death seems to be steeped in mystery and conspiracies that would live on long after him, namely how difficult it was to execute his assassination.

Even before more organized, larger-scale assassination attempts took place, there had been multiple attempts on Rasputin's life. In one instance, in June 1914, a woman ran up to the holy man and stabbed him in the stomach. As she stabbed, she cried out that she did so to protect the innocent from his acts of seduction. Rasputin was severely injured and lost a lot of blood during the attack, but surprisingly, he made a full recovery.

In another assassination attempt, two years after the stabbing, a group of noblemen aimed to rid the tsar of his nefarious companion. Led by Felix Yusupov, a man wed to Nicholas's own niece, Rasputin was invited to what seemed to be a cordial meal in Yusupov's own home. The catch was that Rasputin's portion of dinner, dessert, and even wine was supposedly heavily laced with cyanide, despite later reports showing no cyanide in the monk's system.

Much to the surprise of the group of assassins, as the story goes, Rasputin feasted and drank in excess with no signs of slowing down. If they thought that there was a sufficient amount of cyanide in the food, it must have appeared to them to be a miracle that the monk didn't exhibit any ill effects from the food and the poison housed within it. It was even noted by the assassins later that the immunity that Rasputin seemed to show appeared as though there was some evil force at work, protecting the monk from harm. This likely furthered the men's resolve since it could be interpreted as proof that Rasputin was evil and needed to be removed from the situation.

Not to be deterred, the men pushed forward, shooting Rasputin. By several reports, Rasputin still didn't die right away. Rather, he would be shot several more times and severely beaten before he took his final breaths. Later official reports would state that Rasputin died from a single gunshot to the head.

To make sure the job was done, the assassins threw his corpse in the Malaya Nevka River. Further transforming his demise into legend, there were rumors that when he was pulled out of the river, he was still breathing but later died from his wounds. In reality, Rasputin's body had been frozen in the river before the police found him and retrieved his corpse, which was intact thanks to the extreme temperatures of the Russian winter.

Upon hearing about Rasputin's death, the tsar and tsarina both recoiled in horror. The tsarina seemed to be the most deeply affected, which made sense; her time with Rasputin involved instances of him nursing her son back to health at remarkable speeds and hiding his more lecherous side so that the empress only thought of it as a rumor. Now, Alexandra had lost not only a close friend but also what she believed was the only hope for Alexei's life and his condition.

As for Nicholas, he was leading a staff meeting at the current headquarters for the war when he received the news. He telegraphed back almost immediately, saying that he was "horrified, shaken." There is a suspicion that the persona that Rasputin put on for Nicholas varied greatly from the holy man and healer that he presented himself to Alexandra, as Nicholas would stay another night before he departed to Petrograd on January 1st, 1917—a full day after Rasputin's death.

While Rasputin was far from the shadowy secret leader of Russia that many feared him to be, that didn't mean he was silent on his views to the tsar either. As Rasputin grew closer to the Romanovs, he was less subtle and much louder in his opinions. The tutor and eventually close friend to the imperial family Pierre Gilliard said of the tsar's true opinions on Rasputin near the end of his life, "[He] had tolerated him [Rasputin] because he dared not weaken the Empress's faith in him—a faith that kept her alive. He did not like to send him away, for if Alexei Nicolaievich died, in the eyes of the mother, he would have been the murderer of his own son."

True to form and indicative of the unique and genuine love the two leaders shared, Nicholas went to his wife's side to console her in her time of need. There was no indication that he ever shared with his wife how he truly started to feel about the holy man, and while Rasputin had shown himself to be a nuisance, Nicholas did not want him dead. After all, the tsar loved his family above all else and appreciated Rasputin's seemingly magical ability to bring Alexei back from the brink of death.

Another thing that Nicholas despised and was genuinely disgusted by was the assassins themselves. This time, the assassination of a public figure wasn't carried out by a group of revolutionaries or anyone the tsar could label as a terrorist. Instead, it was members of his own family that had stooped to murder in order to remove someone from the imperial family's sphere whom they didn't like. When asked about the event, he simply said, "I am filled with shame that the hands of my kinsmen are stained with the blood of a simple peasant. A murder is always a murder."

This was a sentiment that much of the royal family shared. Even after the demise of the Romanov Empire, fifty years after the death of Rasputin, Nicholas's sister, Grand Duchess Olga Alexandrovna, carried his message on. She stated:

> There was nothing heroic about Rasputin's murder. It was...premeditated most vilely. Just think of the two names most closely associated with it even to this day—a Grand Duke, one of the grandsons of the Tsar-Liberator, and then a scion of one of our great houses whose wife was a Grand Duke's daughter. That proved how low we had fallen.

Tsar Nicholas made sure to take swift action and punish the assassins immediately while he was still in Petrograd. The conspirators included the ringleader, Yusupov, as well as Grand Duke Dmitri Pavlovich and a right-wing politician named Vladimir Purishkevich.

Yusupov was sentenced to banishment to one of his estates in the center of Russia, but he only stayed there a year before leaving Russia altogether to be with Princess Irina Alexandrovna, Nicholas's niece. Grand Duke Dmitri Pavlovich was sent to join the Russian army, serving his time in Persia. Finally, Purishkevich was allowed to go free without punishment, thanks to his position in the Duma. Punishing Purishkevich would put Nicholas and all of Russia in an even more precarious position than they already occupied.

Interestingly enough, Yusupov's banishment and eventual emigration would eventually save his life. Because of his sentence, he would be out of Russia by the time the Russian Revolution drew near and the royal family was in danger.

Rasputin would be buried on January 3rd, 1917, in the imperial park. While the whole royal family seemed sad at his passing, the empress was especially stricken. One of the funeral attendees stated:

> A closed automobile stopped and the Imperial family joined us. They were dressed in mourning and the Empress carried some white flowers; she was very pale but quite composed although I saw her tears fall when the oak coffin was taken out of the police van...The burial service was read by the chaplain and after the Emperor and Empress had thrown earth on the coffin, the Empress distributed her flowers between the Grand Duchesses and ourselves and we scattered them on the coffin.

This description paints a tragic picture of a pair of leaders who weren't attending a funeral as a publicity stunt or formality, for, despite Rasputin's and Nicholas's differences, they were both genuinely upset at his passing. Again, this can be traced back to a single fact that would haunt almost the entire rule of Nicholas II: the precarious position of his son's health.

The royal family placed two things into Rasputin's coffin. First, there was an idol of the family, signed by both the tsar and tsarina, as well as their children. Alongside it, Alexandra had written a letter to the fallen holy man pleading for help. It read, "My dear martyr, give me thy blessing that it may follow me always on the sad and dreary path I have yet to follow here below. And remember us from on high in your holy prayers."

For Nicholas, though, the death of Rasputin wasn't only the loss of a close family friend and a piece of hope for his wife. Without Rasputin, Russia had lost its final scapegoat. For all of the strife that Rasputin carried with him, he also carried a target on his back. Due to his past and present behavior, he served as an easy person to blame for Russia's misfortune.

Unfortunately, now that Rasputin was dead, there was little that Nicholas could do to deflect the blame off himself. The Duma grew more impatient with Nicholas's military failures, and the people of Russia were growing impatient as well. With many people living in poverty without money for food or even food to buy, much of the population was running out of time as well.

Soon, Nicholas would be faced with a choice: what would he do when revolutionaries rose to a fever pitch? When conflict within Russia threatened to tear the country apart and ruin the efforts of the Russian military on the fronts of World War I? Nicholas was soon approaching a point where he would have to choose what he would put first. Would he choose the needs of Russia that revolutionaries like Lenin were growing ever impatient for, or would he instead opt to behave as he once had, by trying to squash the revolutionary spirit with an autocratic hand much in line with the beliefs of his father, Alexander III?

When push came to shove, Nicholas would be left with a choice: how hard would he have to fight to keep his position in the Russian government? As the revolutionary spirit of Russia increased, paired with the strife caused by and existing on the battlefronts of the largest war in known history at the time, Nicholas would no longer be able to hide behind the title of tsar or avoid criticism.

On March 15th, 1917, Nicholas II would step down as the tsar of Russia and abdicate the throne, opening a new chapter of the Russian Revolution.

Chapter 7 – The Final Years for Nicholas II as Tsar of Russia

After the death of Rasputin, Nicholas opted to stay in Tsarskoe Selo longer. During this time, it started to become even more clear how much the war and unrest in Russia were weighing on the tsar. Whereas people close to him stated that he looked weary before, Nicholas could only be described as completely worn down at this time. A large part of the reason that Nicholas opted to stay in Tsarskoe Selo was for the hope of some kind of tranquility in the midst of a growing storm that was overtaking Europe and Russia.

During his time there, Nicholas limited his visitors. For the most part, he spent much of his personal time in the comfort of his own family. He was noted to hold back from making decisions during this period, whether those decisions concerned his ministers, his troops, or even his subject, who continued to beg for change. The tsar had seemed to grow weary of his position and the stress that was paired with it. After all, Nicholas was a tsar like never before. Not only was he trying to keep Russia in one piece, but he was also trying to handle the country's role in one of the largest military conflicts to date.

That wasn't to say that Nicholas stayed completely away from the information he needed about the army. In fact, during the day,

Nicholas stayed in his own private quarters in Tsarskoe Selo before returning to his family in the evenings. He had turned his billiards room into a map room, where he carefully tracked the movement of the troops.

When Nicholas did receive visitors, they showed growing concern about his appearance. He was noted to be thin and pale. A French diplomat that Nicholas received, Maurice Paléologue, wrote about Nicholas after seeing him at an annual reception on the Russian New Year, stating,

> As usual, Nicholas II was kind and natural and he even affected a certain care-free air; but his pale, thin face betrayed the nature of his secret thoughts. The Emperor's words, his silences and reticences, his grave, drawn features and furtive, distant thoughts and the thoroughly vague and enigmatical quality of his personality, confirm in me...the notion that Nicholas II feels himself overwhelmed and dominated by events, that he has lost all faith in his mission...that he has...abdicated inwardly and is now resigned to disaster.

Another person close to the tsar, former Prime Minister Vladimir Kokovtsov, also recognized these drastic changes as a cause for alarm. Rather than wax introspectively as to what could cause the tsar's change, he was worried about Nicholas's haggard appearance paired with his denial. About the tsar at this time, he said,

> During the year that I had not seen him, he became almost unrecognizable. His face had become very thin and hollow and covered with small wrinkles. His eyes...had become quite faded and wandered aimlessly from object to object...The whites were of a decidedly yellow tinge, and the dark retinas had become colorless, grey, and lifeless...The face of the Tsar bore an expression of helplessness. A forced mirthless smile was fixed upon his lips and he answered, "I am perfectly well and sound, but I spend too much time without exercise and I

am used to much activity. I repeat to you, Vladimir Nicolaievich, I am perfectly alright."

Nicolaievich continued to discuss the tsar's denials in detail. Nicholas claimed that perhaps he hadn't had a good night's sleep or needed a walk and insisted to his visitor that there was no cause for alarm, as he was in perfect condition. Kokovtsov said that he left the meeting in tears, wondering how the tsar could have gotten into such a condition. He fled the room, looking for the grand marshal of the court, Count Paul Benckendorff, as well as the tsar's physician, Dr. Botkin. He begged of them to take note of the tsar's condition and asked them how they couldn't see a health crisis on the horizon.

The two men tried to relieve Kokovtsov of his worries while remaining loyal to the tsar. They insisted that Nicholas wasn't unwell by way of suffering from sickness but rather that the leader was only tired. In other words, they echoed the sentiments of the tsar, promising that, despite all the evidence in front of them saying otherwise, Nicholas was in perfect health. When Kokovtsov left Tsarskoe Selo for Petrograd, he was convinced that Nicholas was "seriously ill and that his illness was of a nervous character."

Soon, as with almost every detail of Nicholas's reign, rumors started to fly about. There were claims that the leader was sick, while others claimed that the tsarina must be giving Nicholas drugs to help him handle the enormous weight on his shoulders. In all likelihood, his appearance and demeanor were caused by the most obvious stressors in his life. The tsar was quite simply, as Paléologue put it, overwhelmed by all that was happening around him, which he was considered responsible for maintaining.

At the same time, Nicholas retreated from the public. His appearances became fewer and further between, and his speeches and letters were sparse. When they did appear, they seemed to hold empty meanings. For instance, in a manifesto primarily written for him by one of his generals, General Iosif Gurko, Nicholas passed on a page full of patriotic phrases without much depth. It read, in part;

The time for peace has not yet come...Russia has not yet performed the tasks this war has set her...The possession of Constantinople and the Straits...the restoration of a free Poland...We remain unshaken in our confidence in victory. God will bless our arms. He will cover them with everlasting glory and give us a peace worthy of your glorious deeds. Oh, my glorious troops, a peace such that generations to come will bless your sacred memory!

While Nicholas likely hoped that these words would come across as soaring, inspiring, and hopeful, they instead left many people scratching their heads. While these words were strong, they lacked substance to give the army direction or command. When Paléologue read these words, he summed up a bleak view of the tsar. "[The manifesto] can only be...a kind of political will, a final announcement of the glorious vision which he had imagined for Russia and which he now sees dissolving into thin air."

There was one person who had the potential to rouse Nicholas from within himself, but she had recently taken a blow as well. Empress Alexandra was noted to have been momentarily crushed by Rasputin's death. After his death, Alexandra was noted to have spent several days crying and, even at times, listlessly staring ahead. However, she was a strong woman, and while she was not quite as powerful as the tsar himself, she was still a leader. Besides, she had a family to care for. She drew on her internal reserves of strength and recalled something that Rasputin told her on multiple occasions: "If I die or you desert me, you will lose your son and your crown within six months."

With this in mind, the tsarina tried to prepare herself for what was going to happen in the coming months. Even if Rasputin hadn't warned her of tragedy ahead, it's likely that the empress felt the ground shaking with the change to come, which almost all Russians could feel at this time.

In addition, while Alexandra couldn't rouse her husband out of his exhaustion, she started to take matters into her own hands. She began to exert herself in political affairs and even make decisions for those around her. She housed her lady-in-waiting, Anna Vyrubova, in the Alexander Palace to offer Anna additional protection from the death threats she'd started to receive since Rasputin's death.

There were signs of Alexandra's influence everywhere. Even in the home they shared, the telephone wasn't meant to sit on Nicholas's desk. Instead, it was moved to her boudoir, where she kept it on a table beneath a picture of Frenchwoman Marie Antoinette.

As for the reports sent to the palace, both Nicholas and Alexandra were given them equally. When Alexander Protopopov, the minister of the interior during the last two years of the Romanov reign, entered the palace, he typically gave the report to whichever one of the heads of states he could find first. Sometimes, the two were even briefed simultaneously rather than Nicholas being pulled to the side separately.

Not one to be left out, Alexandra would often eavesdrop on official conversations between Nicholas and other statesmen. This was something that Nicholas was not only aware of but approved of as well. This was a practice that others would start to pick up on. Not realizing it was the empress who was nearby, Kokovtsov once mentioned in an interview, "I thought that the door leading from the [tsar's] study to his dressing room was half-open, which had never occurred before, and that someone was standing just inside. It may have been just an illusion but this impression stayed with me throughout my brief audience."

Later, the empress would perfect her method of ensuring she was well aware of her husband's affairs and the goings-on in Russia. She did this by installing a staircase that cut through the walls of the estate that led to a small balcony. This allowed the empress to stay up to date on current events while she relaxed on a couch and listened to meetings.

In these ways, the empress was there not only to exercise her own influence but also to prop her husband up when his own leadership started to lag. As always, she was in equal parts asserting her own independence while working on trying to ensure that she outlasted Rasputin's prediction, which stated that with his death, the Romanov family would soon crumble.

When it came to Rasputin's death, the Russian government as a whole didn't change much, likely to the surprise of the conspirators who were convinced that Rasputin's undue influence was secretly controlling Russian affairs.

Another issue that Nicholas had to handle was the continuing revolving door of officials in his government. As time marched on, it seemed that more politicians either refused to serve under Nicholas or argued to the tsar that they were unfit for the role to which they were appointed. At one point, Prince Nikolai Golitsyn, an elderly politician whom both Nicholas and Alexandra supported, begged the tsar to relieve him of his position. Unsuccessfully, he pleaded to the tsar, "If someone else had used the language I used to describe myself, I should have been obliged to challenge him to a duel."

The other minister that the imperial family trusted implicitly, especially the tsarina, was Protopopov, the minister who made sure that Nicholas and Alexandra received regular briefings.

Yet even this minister proved to be a faulty choice. He was incredibly lackluster at his job, and he rarely made an effort to even attend cabinet meetings. As for his relationship with the Duma, he was generally disliked by its members. The Duma president even detailed a New Year's Day reception in which he avoided Protopopov entirely. He later wrote:

> I noticed he was following me...I moved to another part of the hall with my back [to him]. Notwithstanding...Protopopov held out his hand. I replied, "Nowhere and never." Protopopov...took me in a friendly manner by the elbow, saying, "Surely, my dear fellow, we can come to an

understanding." I felt disgusted by him. "Leave me alone. You are repellent to me," I said.

Much like Rasputin before him, Protopopov only held his position because he was in a position of favor with the imperial family, who granted him his political influence without any favor of those outside of their sphere.

If Nicholas and Alexandra comprehended the implications of this issue, they seemed to move past them without a care in the world. The two rulers would continue to handpick their consorts based on little more than personal preference.

However, in a country that was becoming increasingly divided with the voices of revolutionaries growing ever louder, ignoring the court of public opinion would prove fatal to the royal family.

Behind closed doors, though, the facade that the tsar and tsarina tried—and, in Nicholas's case, often failed—to put on for the public started to crumble. Nicholas remained gaunt and disillusioned by the lot he'd been handed as tsar, constantly fretting over the needs of his troops while he tried to keep a fracturing country together under the threat of revolution.

As for the tsarina, Alexandra was noted to frequently spend her evenings staring into the fireplace, listening to music, and generally exuding a joyless air thick with tension. One of the empress's friends, Lili Dehn, joined her one evening only weeks before the political fall of the Romanovs. She asked Alexandra why she was so sad that night, and the leader simply turned around to reply with heavy eyes, "Why am I sad Lili? I can't really say but...I think my heart is broken."

While the tsar and tsarina of Russia may not have been aware of the tragic turn their life would soon take, they did know one thing: they were completely worn down and exhausted. They were leaders who held a challenging position made up of inherited problems that had been boiling for decades, an international conflict that Russia happened to get drawn into, and a whole host of other difficulties that they both directly and indirectly fostered.

Soon, these issues would come to a head in a bloody and brutal overthrow of a monarchy that had existed for a little over three centuries.

Chapter 8 – From Tsar to Citizen: The Abdication of Nicholas II

As tensions rose around Russia, the pressure for Nicholas to take action was overwhelming. Increasingly, the action that people called for was in the form of abdication.

It's crucial to note that, at this point, while some revolutionaries strived for the abolition of the tsarism, these weren't the steps that the ministers around Nicholas were calling for. Instead, they encouraged Nicholas to come to a reasonable deal with the Duma to keep the peace in Russia. There was growing concern that if Russia fell into an all-out revolution in the same vein as the French Revolution, it would cripple the nation, especially on the frontlines of World War I. If Russia collapsed in on itself, the loss of central leadership would also cause the collapse of the military's efforts.

That's why one night, in early March of 1917, Nicholas's Chief of Staff Mikhail Alekseyev sent word to General Nikolai Ivanov, urging him to convince Nicholas to reach a deal with the Duma since the general was to arrive at Tsarskoe Selo the next day. The hope in reaching out to General Ivanov was that Nicholas's lifelong respect for the Russian military and its soldiers would make him more likely to listen to the general, as he no longer listened to his ministers.

Alekseyev would later up the ante and decide that the time had come for Nicholas's reign to end. He dreaded coming across to the tsar as a traitor or disloyal, but he, like many others, feared what the inner turmoil of Russia would do to the war effort. Alekseyev took an extra step when Nicholas was on the way to Pskov and cabled commanders who were active on the front. He asked them before reaching out to the tsar if they agreed that abdication was a reasonable request. He also expressed his fear that the revolutionaries would soon take steps to disrupt Russia's rail network if nothing was changed in their favor and that he feared the possibility of a civil war.

While Alekseyev was worried about the reaction he would receive for his ideas, he was surely met with a mix of emotions, for most of the commanders sent back their agreement. The overwhelming majority had decided that Nicholas's abdication was exactly what the situation called for, as it was too late for reconciliation in Nicholas's personal reign.

With this consensus, Alekseyev sent word to Nicholas in Pskov, informing him of the majority vote and including an additional personal and patriotic plea that the tsar would listen and step down without a fight. To almost everyone's surprise, Nicholas listened. Likely worn down by years of conflict, and seeing reason in the patriotic appeal, he sent a telegram to Alekseyev, stating that he was willing to make whatever sacrifice was called for to save the country he truly loved.

Even with this concession, the official process of abdication had yet to begin. For now, no one was completely sure what steps Nicholas would take.

To expedite the process of abdication, Alekseyev contacted Nikolai Bazili, Nicholas's legal advisor. He urged Bazili to start drafting a manifesto that Nicholas could sign to legally relinquish some of his power before resorting directly to complete abdication. Alekseyev encouraged Bazili to make sure this manifesto gave Mikhail Rodzianko, the conservative State councilor, the power to form a replacement government to make up for the power that Nicholas would give up. Before long, it was decided that even a manifesto of this nature wouldn't be strong enough for the situation. Again, they came to the same severe conclusion: anything that kept Nicholas in power just wouldn't do.

Another suggestion came from Nicholas's cousin, Grand Duke Nicholas Nikolaevich. Rather than a drastic manifesto, Nicholas should simply pass his throne down the natural line of succession. In other words, Tsarevich Alexei, who was only twelve years old at the time, would take the position with his uncle, Nicholas's brother Mikhail, acting as the new tsar's regent. In other words, Mikhail would be the actual leader making the decisions until Alexei was old enough to rule the country in practice rather than as a symbolic figurehead. Still, Nikolaevich avoided directly using the word "abdication." General Brusilov backed up the sentiment, saying that if Nicholas failed to follow this plan, Russia would surely collapse.

As these discussions reached a fever pitch, and as the decisions became more rushed, Nicholas continued to surprise his advisors by agreeing. This was probably in part due to the fact that the empress, who had always encouraged an authoritarian approach, was still in Tsarskoe Selo rather than at Nicholas's side. Many were also surprised at his quick agreement after his reputation for refusing to cooperate with the Duma. As politically and emotionally drained as Nicholas was at the time, the situation likely came at the same moment that Nicholas was ready for the last resort that would relieve him.

Yet there was a bump on the road to abdication. As he prepared to leave the throne to his son, Nicholas consulted a surgeon who had been involved in Alexei's medical care for years, Sergei Fëdorov. He was well trusted by the imperial family because, while he was considered drastic at times, he was knowledgeable, up to date on the latest medical innovations, and had a reassuring bedside manner.

Fëdorov was shocked when Nicholas turned to him for help with one of the most consequential decisions in recent Russian history.

During the conversation, Fëdorov was further shocked by how Nicholas was talking. It seemed to the doctor that Nicholas was harboring the belief Alexei would still live with his parents if he took over the helm of Russian leadership, which was a move that would essentially nullify the effect of Nicholas's abdication, at least in the public eye. When Fëdorov asked Nicholas whether he thought Alexei would live with him, Nicholas responded, "Why ever not? He's still a child and naturally ought to remain inside his family until he's an adult. Until that time, Mikhail Alexandrovich will be regent."

As gently as possible, the doctor told the tsar that this wasn't a situation that he could depend on occurring. He later said Nicholas looked troubled at this realization but quickly changed the subject to Alexei's health, asking if his hemophilia was actually an incurable condition. He told him, "Your Majesty, science tells us that this illness is incurable but many people with it live to a significant age, though Alexei Nikolaevich's health will also always depend on every contingency."

The tsar trailed off and began to speak to himself more than the man in front of him. He made a troubling conclusion for the process of the abdication, saying, "If that's the case, I can't part with Alexei. That would be beyond my powers...and, furthermore, if his health doesn't permit it, then I'll have the right to keep him next to me."

With this realization, a segment of his personality that had emerged before in his reign—his love of family coming before his political decisions and duty to his country – returned to the forefront of his decision-making as his abdication was finalized. In turn, Nicholas tried to make an amendment to his abdication. Rather than the title of tsar being passed to Alexei, it would go to Mikhail, who would then fill the role as the official leader of the country rather than as a regent. As Nicholas saw it, this would still continue the Romanov line while allowing him and Alexandra to keep Alexei safe and close.

There was only one problem: Nicholas wasn't legally allowed to change the line of succession. Even though Nicholas justified his decision with the reasoning that Mikhail was his oldest living relative and was well known for his criticism of his brother, it was still an illegal step for Nicholas to change the line of succession. Mikhail had even served as the living heir between the time that Nicholas had taken the throne until Alexei was born. That didn't change legal precedence, though. Nicholas was well within his rights to abdicate the throne, but the line of succession was set in stone. The law was simple. Tsars could pass on their powers to their heir via death or abdication, but thanks to a law instated in 1796 by Emperor Paul I, they could not change who that heir was. And this was a law that couldn't be changed very easily.

However, Nicholas continued to struggle against the law. It made sense—after all, Nicholas had been raised as an autocrat and ruled as one, so it was new to him to be halted by a simple law. The tsar didn't care that his plan was illegal. He was determined to keep his family intact even if he had to exercise undue authority to do so.

Before long, a party of the tsar's advisors came to appeal to him. When they reached him, they started by pointing out that he may need time to consider the proposal, but Nicholas cut them off, politely but firmly correcting them. He said that he didn't need time to think anything over; he would abdicate, but he wouldn't part with his son. To solve this problem, he would abdicate to his brother.

His advisors tried to convince him of the gravity of the situation if he were to exercise his power in an autocratic manner in his final act as tsar. They continued to explain how Alexei was more than just an heir; he was also a symbol of innocence. As tsar, Alexei could wipe the slate clean for the institution itself and hopefully quell the revolutionary spirits.

Eventually, they conceded, and a document was drafted for Nicholas to abdicate to Mikhail. As they stated it, he was to rule "in complete and unbreakable unity with representatives of the people in legislative institutions."

Shortly after this agreement was made, the tsar retired to his private rooms to make final amendments to the wording of his statement, while one of the attendees of the meeting, Alexander Guchkov, walked outside to see a crowd had gathered. He told them, "Our Father Tsar is in total agreement with us and will do everything that needs to be done."

In response, the crowd took up a rallying cry of excitement, supporting the abdication of the leader that had become so controversial. Later on, after the illegal line of succession was made public, there would be a rumor, potentially based in truth, that members of the party involved in drafting the abdication documentation were unaware of the legal issues revolving around naming a successor other than the lawful heir to the position, Alexei.

Despite this, the deed was finally done. At 11:40 p.m. on March 15th, 1917, Nicholas emerged from his study with an abdication manifesto bearing his signature. For the first time in the little over three centuries of Romanov rule, a tsar had abdicated the throne, and for the most part, the people cheered when the news was delivered to Petrograd that same night. Without conflict, Tsar Nicholas II rescinded his title and became merely a citizen. Acknowledging his loss of power, he immediately sent a message to his brother, reading, "Petrograd. To His Highness—I hope to see you soon, Nicky."

Chapter 9 – A Country in Transition and the Romanovs' Arrest

After resigning from his position as tsar, Nicholas was simply referred to as Nicholas Romanov, another citizen of Russia. This didn't mean that he was treated as just another Russian, though. On March 22nd, 1917, Nicholas would return to his family, who was waiting for him back at Tsarskoe Selo, although this wouldn't go as smoothly as he perhaps hoped.

Alexandra received word of his abdication when it reached Petrograd, which she didn't take well. Once again, her close friend Lili took note of the tsarina's reaction.

> The door opened and the Empress appeared. Her face was distorted with agony, her eyes were full of tears. She tottered rather than walked, and I rushed forward and supported her until she reached the writing table between the windows. She leaned heavily against it and taking my hands in hers, she said brokenly: "Aberdique!" I could not believe my ears. I waited for her next words. They were hardly audible. "The poor dear...all alone down there...what he has gone through, oh my

God, what he has gone through...And I was not there to console him..."

The former empress honestly seemed more heartbroken that she had not been there for Nicholas when he needed her the most. In fact, her following actions were to rush to her family's aid. While Nicholas was on his way back, it was left to Alexandra to comfort her children in the meantime, and she tried to delay their concerns as long as she could. Pierre Gilliard described the unfolding scene in tragic detail. "I saw her in Alexis Nicolaivich's [Alexei Nikolaevich's] room...her face was terrible to see, but with a strength of will which was almost superhuman, she had forced herself to come to the children's rooms as usual so that the young invalids...should suspect nothing."

As Nicholas headed toward the palace to rejoin his family, he called Alexandra to ask if she'd heard the news, to which she only responded with a simple yes. The couple didn't waste any more breath on the loss of their positions. Instead, Nicholas immediately launched into a discussion about the health and welfare of their children.

As for the politics of the situation, Nicholas's abdication seemed to immediately improve the tension in Petrograd. While this wouldn't prove to be the end of the revolution, it did help to ease the overwhelming conflict that had been poised to tear Russia apart. However, there was still conflict afoot. Per Nicholas's abdication agreement, he surrendered the position to Mikhail, who declined the position. This gave the Provisional Government at the time far more power than expected, and they quickly took to installing the reforms they'd long hoped for in the country since the tsar was no longer in the way.

Late at night on March 18th, around ten o'clock, Count Benckendorff received word that the new minister of war under the Provisional Government, Alexander Guchkov, and General Lavr Kornilov were on their way to Tsarskoe Selo to see the former empress. The visitation of Guchkov was particularly alarming because he was formerly known as President Guchkov, the head of the Duma. Put in laymen's terms, he was formerly an enemy of the tsar and tsarina. His presence to the family wasn't seen as a sympathetic visitor and instead heralded red flags indicating a possible arrest of the imperial family. With these worries in mind, Benckendorff immediately sought out Alexandra.

In turn, Alexandra continued the line of communication to Grand Duke Paul Alexandrovich, Nicholas's youngest brother, who hurried from his Tsarskoe Selo home to be at her side. Shortly, only about an hour after Benckendorff had heard the news of the visit, the party arrived. With them were about twenty members of a new council, who was supportive of the revolution.

From here, Alexandra and the grand duke, with little other option, entertained the presence of the party. The council members who accompanied the expected guests were mostly soldiers and workers who were thrilled at the fall of Nicholas. They spent their time in the palace that the tsar's family had been residing in, causing as much havoc as possible. They abused the servants to their heart's content. All the while, they called the inhabitants of the home "bloodsuckers" to make their genuine disdain clear.

As for Kornilov and Guchkov, they arrived together at the palace for their first visit before Nicholas returned, and for good reason. They were there, by their description, to investigate and put the empress and the royal children under the protection of the Provisional Government. For his part, Guchkov remained civil, which the guests he brought with him failed to do. He inquired of Alexandra whether the family had everything they needed; he even made sure to specifically ask if they had all the medicine that they needed on hand, a question that was sure to put Alexandra at ease due to her constant fear of her son's health.

His politeness created some sense of comfort for the former empress, who immediately expressed her relief at his sympathy. She told him that she had all the supplies she needed at the moment, but she did implore the minister of war to check on the hospitals around Tsarskoe Selo, showing her genuine concern for those around her and the state of Russia. She also added a plea that her visitors remain as civil as possible, not for her sake but to ensure that the children remained safe and unalarmed. In turn, Guchkov swore to Alexandra that he would take care of both of these concerns. Later, after returning home, the grand duke would describe to his wife that Alexandra was at her most dignified and tranquil during this visit.

However, the reality behind the situation was that this was the first interaction between a captor and his prisoners. Under the guise of protection, he had taken one of the first steps toward putting Alexandra and the Romanov children under arrest.

Despite her calm demeanor, Alexandra wasn't a gullible woman. She saw the threat on the horizon and took measures to prevent the worst from happening. Lili Dehn would later describe Alexandra's actions as being prudent, as she took care to burn her diaries and letters so they couldn't be against her later. The only letters saved from the chaos were the correspondence shared between Alexandra and Nicholas, perhaps partially from how cherished their relationship was to Alexandra but more likely as evidence to be saved for the trial, which was something that people were already beginning to whisper about. With these letters, evidence of their genuine love for Russia and their patriotic spirit was preserved, making the pair look less selfish in the eyes of a court. Dehn would describe the night, saying, "A fierce fire was burning in the huge grate in the red drawing room...She reread some of them...I heard stifled sobs...Still weeping, she laid her letters one by one on the heart of the fire. The writing glowed for an instance...then it faded and the paper became a little heap of white ash."

Nicholas had yet to return home at this point. For now, the abdicated ruler knew not what was happening to his family.

Interestingly and unfortunately, while the revolution in Russia reached the levels that the revolutionaries had dreamed of for years, the strategic move of abdication didn't have the effect on the army that Nicholas and his generals had hoped for. The first order of the new Petrograd Soviet allowed soldiers some freedom to elect their superiors, as the leadership was overhauled. This led to a new round of confusion rather than the unity that Nicholas hoped his abdication would bring to the frontlines.

This allowed the revolutionary spirit that had been at the heart of Russia to spread to the troops on the frontlines. Many who were loyal to the tsar saw the abdication as a betrayal, while other soldiers took advantage of the chaos to slack in their performance and even lessen their discipline in their work and to their superior officers.

Loyalty for the tsar was so strong that the Chevalier Guards left their squadron's station in Novgorod and took it upon themselves to rush to the tsar's aid. The Russian winter proved too harsh for this task, and two days later, they arrived from the front, exhausted, only to find that they had abandoned their post without reason. It was too late. Nicholas had already left the sacred role of the tsar.

A second visit to Alexandra came from General Kornilov only a day before Nicholas was to return. When he reached the palace, Alexandra was well aware of his mission, for she knew that the general was there to issue her family's arrest. While she received him, now in the uniform of a nurse rather than the elegant garb of a tsarina, she stayed stone-faced as he explained his purpose. For a woman who had been raised to be a gracious leader, the former tsarina looked her captor in the eye, refused to hold out a hand to him, and didn't show any weakness of emotion in his presence. The sobbing woman who had rid the palace of evidence was gone. Now, Kornilov looked into the eyes of a tough woman who wouldn't break, even if her husband's political opponents planned to come for his family before his return.

As for Kornilov, he tried to put the family at ease with a light explanation of the arrest. This wasn't a piece of political retribution by the Provisional Government, at least by his description, but rather a move made for the safety of the Romanov family.

This explanation was enough for Alexandra. Her initial resolve faded throughout his visit, and the two retreated from an icy standoff to a more familiar relationship, as the two sat at a table in the drawing room.

At the same time that Alexandra was being informed of the arrest in Tsarskoe Selo, Nicholas was at Mogilev, almost 770 kilometers (about 478 miles) away Here, he was also arrested and fed the same explanation, that the arrest was a precaution on his behalf. Nicholas and Alexandra were informed that they would be reunited the next day when Nicholas returned to the palace.

After the former leaders were informed of their fate, the arrest was announced on a wider scale, starting with Kornilov relieving the guards who had been protecting the tsar and tsarina at Tsarskoe Selo. New soldiers would come to take their place and serve as prison guards for Nicholas, Alexandra, and the rest of the family. Proving how far the arrest would go, and testing the loyalty of the men in front of him, the general gave the men a choice as to the end of their tenure at Tsarskoe Selo. If the men left, they were free to go so long as they never returned to the palace. If they wanted to support the former tsar and stay, they were also welcome to do that, but they would be placed under arrest alongside the Romanov family. While some close to the royal family, such as Alexandra's close companions and the children's tutor Pierre Gilliard, remained, most of the men working as guards at the palace deserted for their own safety. Once these posts were occupied by the new, harsher guards, the house arrest of the Romanovs would officially start.

With the downward spiral that the Romanovs seemed to be locked into, as well as the obvious changes in the household, it was time that the children were informed as to what had happened. Alexandra sent Alexei's tutor, Gilliard, to explain the news to him, while Alexandra herself went to her daughters.

Gilliard went to the former tsarevich and broke down what had happened in a way that the young boy would understand. He was particularly impressed that Alexei didn't once ask about his position as heir. Instead, he asked of his father's welfare and wondered who would rule Russia. The tutor explained to the boy that he'd be with his father soon, and for now, all that he knew—which was all that anyone in Russia knew—was that the Provisional Government had taken the reins.

That evening, the doors of Tsarskoe Selo were locked. This time, they weren't to bar out anyone who might bear ill will for the Romanov family for their safety but to keep the former imperial family locked into the palace.

On the morning of March 22nd, Alexandra and her children waited with bated breath. They were told that Nicholas, who had simply been traveling home and was now under arrest, would arrive. With recent events in mind, no one in the family was completely sure that the promised return of their beloved father figure would come true. Much to their relief, and right on time, a train pulled into the station and out came Nicholas—whose travels were largely undocumented—and he was passed over from the officers responsible for his arrest to the palace commander.

As he arrived back at the palace, Nicholas was purposely humiliated when he drove up to the locked gates. He pled for entry as an officer repeatedly made him state who he was, seeming to pretend to not recognize the name of the man who was once considered to be the most important man in all of Russia. When he finally walked into the palace, the once-saluted leader was greeted with casual guards who were relaxing, smoking, or simply watching Nicholas pass. He returned the empty gesture by tipping his hat in a faux return salute before continuing inside. This event would set the tone for Nicholas and his family's arrest. The earlier frustrations of their captors would be taken out on the former royals to make their transition from tsar and tsarina to citizens as painful as possible.

At long last, Nicholas had returned to his beloved wife and children. The couple retreated to one of the children's rooms for a moment alone. Alexandra made sure it was clear to her husband that her praise over the years wasn't to boost the ego of a nervous tsar who seemed unready and unprepared to rule. Crying, she pled for him to believe her when she said that she didn't love him only for his role in government but adored and admired him as her husband and the father to their children. In not so many words, she promised Nicholas that she was there for him and would be there for him on their rocky road ahead. She would be there with him until the bitter end.

With his wife before him offering the same love she had offered him when they met as teenagers, and away from the prying eyes of the officers of the Provisional Government, Nicholas finally broke down after years of exhaustion and in recognition of the dire situation in which his family now found themselves. Alone, locked in their palace that had been quickly converted from a place of political power into a makeshift prison, Nicholas laid his head on his wife's chest, held her closely, and wept.

Chapter 10 – The Execution of Nicholas II and the Romanov Family

As he acclimated to his new imprisonment, Nicholas made sure to seek out Lili Dehn and thank her for her service and her close friendship to Alexandra. Without a country to rule, Nicholas quickly fell into the role that he was more naturally made for: a patriarch in his family. And he was set on doing whatever he could to ensure their safety and comfort against the nearly insurmountable odds that they faced.

His years as the tsar, especially the last few months, which placed an unprecedented amount of stress on Nicholas, had taken a toll on him. Even if he was relieved to be free of the role that he once proclaimed he wasn't ready for, he was still a prisoner and was worried about the safety of his family who was imprisoned alongside him. He wore the stress in the sudden lines on his face and in his strikingly gray hair. Lili would write a shocking account of the appearance of Nicholas, who she had seen regularly not so long ago. "The Emperor was deathly pale. His face was covered with innumerable wrinkles, his hair was quite grey at the temples, and blue shadows encircled his eyes. He looked like an old man."

As the imprisonment of the Romanovs went on, it became obvious, at least from a retrospective view, that the move was sudden and not completely planned out. While officials made the immediate move to place the former rulers and their family under arrest, there was a serious lack in planning as to what to do with the Romanovs from here on out.

Nicholas sought out his captors to question the fate of his family. When he spoke to Count Benckendorff, he was told that there were arrangements for the family made through General Kornilov. Initially, the plan was to keep the family locked in their palace indefinitely as prisoners. There were exceptions to this strict imprisonment, though. Namely, an area of the park directly outside of the palace was open for the family to use whenever Nicholas wanted to spend some time outdoors in the fresh air.

Still, even with this exception, the movement of the family was closely monitored. If Nicholas wished to walk in the park, it had to be prearranged so that guards were available to be present. Again, this was to drive home the point that Nicholas and his family were no longer royals, a point that would make their lives more difficult and embarrassing. If they wanted to go out, the family, who once had an army of servants at their beck and call to cater to their every whim, had to wait close to a half an hour or more for someone to bring a key to allow them to leave.

Even while he tried to enjoy his short time outdoors, his wife, Lili, and another ally of Alexandra named Anna Vyrubova watched nervously from the window to see what would happen when Nicholas was left alone with the guards. It wouldn't be long before these onlookers would watch in horror as he was stopped by half a dozen armed guards, who were ready to make the former tsar's life as miserable as possible. Anna recorded:

With their fists and with the butts of their guns they pushed the Emperor this way and that as though he were some wretched vagrant they were baiting on a country road. "You can't go there, Mr. Colonel." "We don't permit you to walk in that direction, Mr. Colonel." "Stand back when you are commanded, Mr. Colonel." The Emperor, apparently unmoved, looked from one of these coarse brutes to another and with great dignity turned and walked back to the palace.

To his supporters imprisoned with him, this instance demonstrated a couple of things to them. For one, it showed that Nicholas would remain as dignified as possible, even when the guards goaded him to fight. Alexandra, for her part, stood silently in the window, gripping Lili's hand as she watched her husband suffer this harsh treatment. Lili would also note a second realization as the women stood in the window, watching the situation unfold. "I do not think that until this moment we had realized the crushing grip of the Revolution but it was brought home to us most forcibly, when we saw the passage of the Lord of All the Russias, the Emperor whose domains extended over millions of miles, now restricted to a few yards in his own park."

As stricken as the silent sentinels were and as doubtlessly frustrated and humiliated as Nicholas was, the abuse that these prisoners would endure had only just begun. There was a long road ahead for the Romanovs, and it was riddled with mistreatment that largely came at the hands of soldiers who finally saw a chance to take out their frustrations on the former tsar and his family. For the most part, whatever the guards did to the Romanovs, they simply had to bear it. As for Nicholas, he chose to retain an air of composure, likely both encouraged by an upbringing of formal etiquette and an effort to maintain the remainder of his self-image by not devolving into the fights he was being goaded into. It's also likely that Nicholas's behavior was, in large part, influenced by his desire to try and keep his family's hopes up against all the odds.

Another sign of the disarray regarding the Romanovs, at least as far as the Petrograd Soviet went, would come shortly. Occurring on the evening of Nicholas's tumultuous outing, a group of soldiers appeared at the gates of the palace, commanding for Nicholas to be turned over to them. Their plan was to remove Nicholas from his family and condemn him to a prison cell within the Peter and Paul Fortress, which would later be turned into a prison, complete with an execution ground, years after the Bolsheviks rose to prominence. The intruders came to a compromise: if they could see Nicholas, they would allow him to remain at the palace. To keep the tentative peace, Benckendorff agreed to the so-called inspection of the former tsar's imprisonment. He documented it as follows:

> I found the Emperor with his sick children, informed him of what had happened, and begged him to come down and walk slowly along the long corridor...He did this a quarter of an hour later. In the meantime, the Commandant, all the officers of the Guard...and myself, stationed ourselves at the end of the corridor so as to be between the Emperor and [the invaders]. The corridor was lit up brightly, the Emperor walked slowly from one door to the other and... [the leader of the intruders] declared himself satisfied. He could, he said, reassure those who sent him.

As the tensions about the Romanovs' fate rose in the newfound Soviet, the conditions of the family themselves started to decline. The children, as Benckendorff documented in his account, were stricken with illness. The two doctors imprisoned with the family, Vladimir Derevenko and Eugene Botkin, worked their best to handle the measles that were sweeping through the family, which posed a particular threat to Maria Romanov, as she was stricken the hardest.

The family was also fairly cut off from the outside world. All of the letters going in and out of the palace were obviously read by the guards to maintain their deep control over the goings-on in the palace, and all but one telephone line in the house was cut. The final working telephone was, naturally and conveniently, in the guards' room, where every word that the royals spoke were monitored. The guards even had to be persuaded by the doctors that they should be allowed to treat Grand Duchess Maria without their prying eyes directly looking over the doctor and his patient.

The guards also weren't afraid to take advantage of the lack of control the family held over them. Soldiers took chairs from within the palace so that they could sit comfortably at their post rather than stand at attention. At least in part to capitalize on the annoyance that Nicholas took in it, the guards sported a disheveled appearance, which was the antipathy of the image Nicholas once commanded of his army. With their shaggy hair and unbuttoned jackets, they took every opportunity to make Nicholas's life as difficult as possible.

Nicholas had to suffer, as he watched the abuse against him extend to his family as well. Even the baby of the family, unwell Alexei, wasn't safe from the mistreatment. At the hands of one of his former "sailor nannies," who were meant to protect him, Alexei was seen being ordered around to do even the most menial tasks and cater to his protector-turned-tormentor's every whim.

The family tried to push on despite these conditions. Once the Romanov children were no longer too ill, the parents used the remaining people in the palace to resume the children's studies. Even Nicholas took on the role of tutor for the subject of history, and in his continuing effort to keep the atmosphere as light as possible, he greeted fellow tutors such as Pierre Gilliard as his "colleague."

Nicholas's often-light attitude in the face of such a situation was controversial within the palace walls. To his enemies, the fact that Nicholas hadn't fallen into an irrevocable depression wasn't the emotional blow they had hoped to deal out to him. As their disdain for his demeanor grew, those who were close to the fallen leader saw this as Nicholas taking advantage of the one thing he'd always hoped for: more time with his family. The power that Nicholas had been saddled with, that he never truly wanted, was gone, and he was free to do as he pleased.

For the first time since Nicholas was young, there wasn't anything expected of him. He wasn't scheduled to meet with ministers all day or balance his power against the Duma's. He was allowed to live as he pleased within the restrictions of imprisonment. Nicholas could start his day with his Bible rather than a briefing, and he often chose to spend his days with his children.

His humor would even lift Alexandra's spirits, who now sported a head of gray hair and moved around the palace with Nicholas pushing her wheelchair, as she had been weakened both by the bout of measles and by the immensely stressful situation she found herself and her family in. She failed to adjust to her new, restricted lifestyle, but she could still smile when her husband made efforts to keep spirits up.

Even above his love of family was his love for Russia. Nicholas was willing to endure whatever he had to as long as he knew that the new rulers would save Russia in a way that he couldn't. As those around him stated, Nicholas was deeply patriotic, and he was ready to do whatever was needed to keep Russia strong. Gilliard would describe Nicholas as an anchor for the prisoners in the palace:

> The Tsar accepted all these restraints with extraordinary serenity and moral grandeur. No word of reproach ever passed his lips. The fact was that his whole being was dominated by one passion, which was more powerful even than the bonds between himself and his family - his love of country. We felt that he was ready to forgive everything to those who were inflicting such humiliations upon him so long as they were capable of saving Russia.

While Nicholas might have been keeping spirits as high as could be expected to those under house arrest in the palace, those back in Petrograd weren't appreciative of his presence. In fact, even well after his abdication and arrest, disapproval and even hatred toward the former tsar were constantly on the rise. Rumors even took hold that Nicholas and Alexandra would betray Russia to Alexandra's home country of Germany in an attempt to try to regain their power in the form of a restored autocracy. One of Nicholas's favorite jokes that Alexandra later picked up on was that he wasn't to be called the tsar anymore but by his real title, "Ex," as in the "Ex-Tsar."

Despite the fact that this was far from the minds of the former rulers, the media picked up the story, and quickly, a second wave of distaste for the Romanovs was whipped up. Additional theories flew around as to the living conditions of the imprisoned family. Some tabloids would claim that the family was gorging themselves on the finest food when, in reality, the family was actually served meals that included soured meat.

In light of these accusations, the Soviet sent one of their chief revolutionaries, Alexander Kerensky, to inspect the living conditions of Nicholas and his family. His job was to see if there were grounds to throw Nicholas in the Peter and Paul Fortress, which was something the Soviet was increasingly demanding. At the end of an eighteen-day investigation, Kerensky declared that, while he learned little from the former tsar and tsarina as to why they made the decisions they did as the rulers, he didn't find any signs of treason. There were no signs that betrayal was on Nicholas's and Alexandra's minds.

There were a number of ideas floating around as to what to do with the royal family. Some views, such as those held by Kerensky, saw the Romanov family as relatively unthreatening. They championed the idea that the Romanovs should leave Russia, but they did not believe that the family should be executed. There was a briefly held idea that the family could be sent to England to live out the rest of their days in exile. Some proponents of this even called upon the early reasons for their arrest, saying that it would be for the sake of the tsar's safety and allow the family more freedom.

There were proponents for this idea who saw this as more than a way to secure the freedom of Nicholas and his family. They knew that sending the tsar away to England was potentially the last chance to save his life as well.

The opponents of this concept still harbored a fear that Nicholas and Alexandra would either betray Russia or be rescued by their old allies, who still held power in the post-World War I world. In the end, the disdain and outright fear of the Romanovs is what sealed their fate.

The Romanovs would go through several location changes as they reached the end of their lives. First, in August of 1917, the family was relocated from Tsarskoe Selo to Tobolsk, Siberia. The family was told, yet again, that this was to protect them from the rising tide of opposition, which was only growing with the waves of revolution sweeping through Petrograd. During this time, they lived in a mansion that had once been used by a governor, and so, as far as their accommodations went, their condition didn't change too drastically from their previous abode. Back at the capital city, the movement pushing to put Nicholas on trial grew stronger every day.

Finally, the Romanovs were removed from Tobolsk and sent to Yekaterinburg, Russia. This time, the family's evacuation was broken up. Nicholas and Alexandra left first alongside their daughter Maria. Due to complications with his hemophilia, Alexei was too ill to travel and stayed behind with his other sisters, Anastasia, Tatiana, and Olga. By May 1918, the children would be reunited with their parents at the Ipatiev House, which was smaller than Tsarskoe Selo but was still an expansive mansion estate compared to the average Russian home. This was where the family stayed until July 17th, 1918.

On this day, the family was awakened early in the morning and given immediate orders to go to the basement of the building they'd been living in for just about two months. Unbeknownst to them, the Bolsheviks had made the final decision as to the sentence of the Romanov family: they were all to be executed. This decision would prove controversial, as those who gave the orders did so discreetly; for instance, they carried out the sentence early in the morning. This also took place only hours after the decision had been made.

The family simply followed the orders with little question. Still in their nightclothes, the Romanovs descended to the basement. Nicholas was even carrying the half-asleep Alexei, while Anastasia was holding her spaniel in her arms. While they were requested to wait, Nicholas asked the man who was soon to be his executioner, Yakov Yurovsky, for chairs for his family. These were brought down, allowing Alexandra, Nicholas, and Alexei to rest. Behind these chairs, the Romanov sisters stood in a line, awaiting whatever order they'd been woken up to answer.

Shortly thereafter, a firing squad would arrive in the room. In carrying out the sentence, Yurovsky stated, "Your relations have tried to save you. They have failed and we must now shoot you."

Too shocked to act fully, Nicholas would only utter a simple "What?" as his last word. In answer, Yurovsky repeated what he said, raised his revolver, and shot Nicholas in the head. This was the signal that the firing squad was waiting for, and they immediately fired. Alexandra made the sign of the cross in a final act of religiosity before following her husband's fate, and three of the sisters, Maria, Olga, and Tatiana, were killed by the first round of bullets.

When the firing squad had emptied their clips, only Alexei and Anastasia drew breath, alongside the spaniel and the family maid. For their luck, they were repaid with an even more brutal death. They were beaten to death and stabbed with bayonets, and eventually, some of the executioners would reload to end the prolonged affair. The Romanovs' maid, who had been included in the order, ended up dying as she screamed in terror and ran about the basement, desperate for escape, although there wasn't any hope for such a thing. Her body bore over thirty stab wounds from the bayonets of her executioners by the time she drew her last breath. Even Anastasia's poor spaniel, Jimmy, was bludgeoned to death with the butt of a rifle.

Even after this, as the gun smoke cleared and blood stained the basement floor, a small sound was heard. Shockingly, it was feeble Alexei who was still alive, still laying in his dead father's arms. In turn, the executioners savagely stomped on the young boy's face, followed by another soldier delivering two bullets to his head. At the sight of this cruelty, a single scream was heard from Anastasia, who had lost and regained consciousness during the mayhem. Her sound brought the attention of the entire squad, and they all attacked her, making her death far more brutal than was necessary.

With the final grand duchess in the room now officially dead, the executioners had to dispose of the corpses that now filled the basement room. After over 300 years on the throne and a tumultuous revolution, the Romanov family was dead in an execution that lasted less than twenty minutes. Peter Gilliard, who only barely missed the execution thanks to his Swiss citizenship, would carry the memory of the family with him for the rest of his life. "I keep a memory of the horrible events that I witnessed, deep in my soul. I saw one of the greatest empires in the world falling, side by side with its monarchs."

Conclusion: The Legacy of Nicholas II

On July 25th, 1918, only approximately a week after the execution of the Romanovs, a group known as the White Russians, members of the Russian White Army, would arrive at the last known safehouse that the family had occupied. This group was made up of anti-communists and individuals opposed to the Russian Revolution who supported Nicholas and Alexandra. Their goal upon arriving was to help the Romanovs escape to freedom, but when they arrived, they found a scene they weren't expecting. For once they arrived, there weren't any Romanovs to save.

They didn't find bodies littered in a basement but rather just an empty house that seemed long abandoned. Unbeknownst to them, the Romanovs' bodies had been taken from the scene of their execution shortly after the act was carried out. Yurovsky and the men assigned to aid him in the execution had stripped the Romanovs of their clothes and threw them unceremoniously into a pair of shallow graves nearby. The executioners would even go so far as to remove the jewels that the imperial family had sewn into their clothes, as they had held onto the hope that they would escape, or, at the very least, the younger members of the family would have the chance to escape. This is most likely why Anastasia survived for so long, as the bullets would have simply ricocheted off the hidden jewels. One grave would hold Nicholas and Alexandra, as well as three of their children, likely their daughters Olga, Tatiana, and Maria. In the second grave lay two smaller corpses, likely the bodies of Anastasia and Alexei.

The execution of the Romanov family wasn't immediately made public, leading to decades of speculation and rumor. Over the years, there were claims that the Romanovs escaped their imprisonment to live out the rest of their years in relative freedom and peace, even if they had to do so in hiding. Even as claims of the execution began to surface, the lack of concrete proof of the family's death was a breeding ground for conspiracy theories. Even though some people believed that Nicholas and Alexandra had fallen victim to a Bolshevik firing squad, many remained unsure about the fates of the children. Much of this was likely under the hopeful disbelief that even if the adult Romanovs had been executed, there was no way that the Bolsheviks would have ordered the deaths of the children.

As the years carried on, multiple individuals would come forward to claim that they were members of the Romanov family. The most popular claim was among women who swore that they were Anastasia. Many of these claims were disproven even before the bodies of the former imperial family were exhumed, but it was a phenomenon that would keep the Romanovs in the public eye decades after their deaths and add to the mystery and conspiracy that shrouded the family.

For a long time, Nicholas remained the villain in the revolutionaries' story. On his shoulders, even decades after his death, were placed famine, poverty, and the countless deaths of the Russian Empire. Doubtlessly, many of his decisions did lead to chaos and ruin. Later, though, this would grow to be attributed less to his cold heart and selfish autocratic ways and instead to the evidence that showed that Nicholas was woefully unprepared to take charge of the country. Not only did his father, Tsar Alexander III, neglect to teach him much of what many tsareviches before him learned, but Nicholas was also a leader crippled by self-doubt. He showed a tendency to surround himself with people who agreed with him, both because of his autocratic leanings and because he needed his decisions bolstered before he had the confidence to make them. These are traits that led to the uniquely heavy influence of Empress Alexandra on what was considered her husband's birthright leadership role.

Nicholas was also in the unique position of inheriting the leadership of a country that was already experiencing unrest. While his father may have crushed the revolutionaries with a heavy hand, it was an act of a hopeful, if not misguided, revolutionary that took the throne from Alexander II and passed it down to Alexander III.

Because of this, Nicholas was set to bear the weight of a country dissatisfied with a 300-year-old ruling system, which was at the helm of a number of different oppressions that inspired change. As the revolutionary spirit of the Russians grew every day he held the title of tsar, and even beyond his abdication, he was the well-timed figurehead who would bear the burden of not only the problems of his own creation but also of those that were already in place before he took on the mantle.

Even today, to say that Nicholas is viewed as a purely good or bad leader of Russia would be a distortion of his legacy rather than a revived look at it. However, by considering the personality of the last tsar and the events that shaped him into the leader he was, the world has been able to look back on Nicholas with new eyes. Most historians now don't solely place the blame on Nicholas for the Russian Revolution and the rise of the Soviet Union and Vladimir Lenin. However, they do recognize that he played a significant role in fostering a state in which those revolutionary opinions were primed to take hold. He wasn't a martyr who died due to a gross misunderstanding of his innocence, but he also wasn't a purely evil leader who put the expansion of his own power over the good of Russia at every possible chance either.

At best, Nicholas is remembered today as a flawed leader. He represents a chapter of history in which he was unable to rule effectively, both by his own doing and by others. While part of his lack of leadership skills can be attributed to poor training, he was also a leader who often failed to compromise and thus lacked the ability to lead a more peaceful reformation of the Russian government.

It wasn't until 1991, when the Soviet Union collapsed, that the truth about the end of Nicholas's and his family's life would come to light. This was when the two mass graves that had been waiting to be discovered since 1918 would be found and their contents exhumed. Thanks to advances in science and the modern practice of DNA testing, it quickly became clear that the mystery that had shrouded the Romanov name for decades was finally solved, even if the answer was steeped in tragedy. Nicholas himself wasn't even the saddest part of the discovery to many; rather, it was the execution of the children, as the youngest children's lives were cut down at the ages of nineteen and twenty-one.

As more details about the execution came out, further sympathy was aroused when the public learned of the brutal methods in which the family died.

All in all, the way the public has viewed Nicholas II has come out of an increasing number of details about his life, his personal correspondence, and the eyewitness accounts of those around him. While the early Soviet Union labeled him as a bloodthirsty monster and a savage with the goal of only increasing his own level of power, further evidence proves otherwise.

While some of the exact details of the tsar's life are conflicting, there are clear threads that prove he was a devoted father, husband, and, by many accounts, a staunch patriot who wanted the best for Russia—even if that meant resigning from his position of power.

The full picture of Nicholas II paints him as a much more conflicted historical figure than he was propagandized as by the revolutionary party in Russia. While deeply flawed, Nicholas II neither represents pure good or pure evil, just as many historical figures before and after him.

In recent years, polls in Russia about Nicholas II have shown a much higher approval rating than public opinion during and especially near the end of his reign. With time and new information, as well as separation from the issues that elicited strong emotions and reactions from both sides of the debate in Russia in the early 1900s, positive opinions of Nicholas's reign began to emerge. This was likely helped by the more neutral posturing of the facts.

Nicholas and, in particular, Alexandra would be pleased to see that, decades later, the figureheads of their faith would offer the family post-mortem redemption. In 2000, the Russian Orthodox Church officially canonized the Romanov family as saints. This process, known within the Russian Orthodox Church as glorification, elevated them to sainthood under the title of passion bearers, as they were the victims of oppression at the hands of the Bolsheviks.

Bibliography

"Bloody Sunday 1905." Alphahistory.com, February 11, 2020. https://alphahistory.com/russianrevolution/bloody-sunday-1905/.

Harris, Carolyn. "The Murder of Rasputin, 100 Years Later." Smithsonian.com. Smithsonian Institution, December 27, 2016. https://www.smithsonianmag.com/history/murder-rasputin-100-years-later-180961572/.

Hasic, Albinko. "Rasputin: 5 Myths and Truths About the Mystic Russian Monk." Time. Time, December 29, 2016. https://time.com/4606775/5-myths-rasputin/.

"Kaiser Wilhelm of Germany and Czar Nicholas of Russia Exchange Telegrams." History.com. A&E Television Networks, July 25, 2019. https://www.history.com/this-day-in-history/kaiser-wilhelm-of-germany-and-czar-nicholas-of-russia-exchange-telegrams.

Massie, Robert K. Nicholas and Alexandra: The Classic Account of the Fall of the Romanov Dynasty. 3. Vol. 3. Ballantine Books, 1967.

Mosse, W.E. "Alexander II." Encyclopedia Britannica. Encyclopedia Britannica, Inc., April 25, 2020. https://www.britannica.com/biography/Alexander-II-emperor-of-Russia.

"Nicholas II." Biography.com. A&E Networks Television, May 19, 2015. https://www.biography.com/royalty/nicholas-ii.

"Russo-Japanese War." History.com, March 23, 2018. https://www.history.com/topics/korea/russo-japanese-war.

Service, Robert. *The Last of the Tsars: Nicholas II and the Russian Revolution.* Pegasus Books, 2017.

Shapiro, Ari. "The Shifting Legacy of the Man Who Shot Franz Ferdinand." NPR. NPR, June 27, 2014. https://www.npr.org/sections/parallels/2014/06/27/326164157/the-shifting-legacy-of-the-man-who-shot-franz-ferdinand.

Tsar Nicholas II: A Life from Beginning to End. Hourly History, 2017.

Yegrov, Oleg. "Imprisoned with the Romanovs: The Story of a Very Unlucky French Tutor." Rbth.com. Russia Beyond. July 17, 2019. https://www.rbth.com/history/330676-pierre-gilliard-romanovs-french-tutor-swiss

Here's another book by Captivating History
that you might be interested in

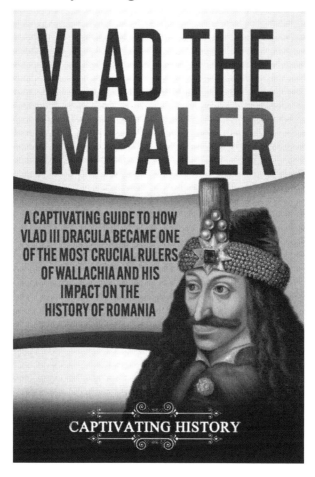

Printed in Great Britain
by Amazon

58298871R00064